C0-AKZ-794

MATH IN A CULTURAL CONTEXT

Building a Fish Rack

Investigations into Proof, Properties, Perimeter, and Area

Grade 6

Barbara L. Adams
Jerry Lipka

Developed by University of Alaska Fairbanks, Fairbanks, Alaska

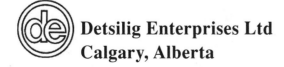
Detsilig Enterprises Ltd
Calgary, Alberta

Building a Fish Rack: Investigations into Proofs, Properties, Perimeter, and Area
© 2003 University of Alaska Fairbanks

National Library of Canada Cataloguing in Publication Data

Adams, Barbara L.

Building a fish rack : investigations into proofs, properties, perimeter, and area / Barbara L. Adams and Jerry Lipka.

(Math in a cultural context: lessons learned from Yup'ik Eskimo elders)

Includes bibliographical references.

ISBN 1-55059-258-0

1. Mathematics—Study and teaching (Elementary) 2. Yupik Eskimos—Study and teaching (Elementary) I. Lipka, Jerry. II. Title. III. Series.

QA135.6.A32 2003   372.7'044   C2003-910484-2

Math in a Cultural Context: Lessons Learned from Yup'ik Eskimo Elders© was developed at the University of Alaska Fairbanks. This work was supported in part by the National Science Foundation Grant No. 9618099 and the project's title was Adapting Yup'ik Elders' Knowledge: Pre-K-to-6th Math and Instructional Materials Development.

All rights reserved. No part of this book may be reproduced in any form or by any means without permission in writing from the publisher. The publisher grants limited reproduction permission for classroom teachers and aides for the purposed of making copies for overhead transparencies, student worksheets, handouts, student coloring book, and similarly related in-class student work.

This project was sponsored, in part, by the National Science Foundation
Opinions expressed are those of the authors and not necessarily those of the Foundation

This project was also sponsored, in part, by the University of Alaska Fairbanks
Alaska Schools Research Fund and the Bristol Bay Curriculum Project

Detselig Enterprises Ltd. acknowledges the financial support of the Government of Canada through the Book Publishing Industry Development Program (BPIDP) for our publishing activities. We also acknowledge the support of the Alberta Foundation for the Arts for our publishing program.

Detselig Enterprises Ltd.
210-1220 Kensington Rd. N.W., Calgary, AB, T2N 3P5
Phone: (403) 283-0900/Fax: (403) 283-6947/E-mail: temeron@telusplanet.net
www.temerondetselig.com

ISBN: 1-55059-258-0
SAN: 115-0324
Printed in Canada.

MATH IN A CULTURAL CONTEXT

MCC

Principal Investigator and Series Editor:
Jerry Lipka
Project Mathematicians:
Barbara L. Adams and Susan Addington
Project Manager: Flor Banks
Project Illustrator: Putt (Elizabeth) Clark
Project Layout: Sarah McGowan, Beverly
Peterson, Sue Mitchell
Project Yup'ik Educational Consultants: Mary
George, Ferdinand Sharp, Evelyn Yanez

Evaluation and Assessment
Jo Ann Izu
Kay Gilliland

Folklorist
Ben Orr

**Graduate Research Assistants
and Classroom Observers**
Randi Berlinger
Hannibal Grubis
Dominique Meierotto
Sandra Wildfeuer

Math Consultants
Claudette Bradley-Engblom
Tod Shockey
Sandra Wildfeuer

Yup'ik Elders and Consultants
Henry Alakayak
Frederick George
Mary George
Jonah Lomack
Sam Ivan
George Moses
Joshua Phillip
Ferdinand Sharp
Mike Toyukak

Technical Support
Dennis Schall

Teachers Piloting the Module
Jared Ahlberg
Travis Ahlberg
Mechelle Andrews
Larry Bartman
Mark Biberg
Bob Bordelon
Stacy Clark
Jon Clouse
Lillian Dimmitt
Leslie Dolan
Tom Dolan
Kimberly Grimes
Alice Hoffman
Clayton Holland
Eleanor Hungate
Jeff Jacobson
Thad Keener
Daniel Klein
Marcy Kuntz
Doreen Lacy
Felicia Leipzig
Mike McGill
Elizabeth Medina
Doug Noon
Chip Nordhoff
Janice Olsen
Jeanne Perkins
DeBorah Snoderly
Janet Speed
Cath Steger
Karen Wiley

Technical Editing
Marie Beaver
Snježana Dananić
Ericka Iseri
Sue Mitchell
Katherine Mulcrone
T. J. O'Donnell

Yup'ik Translators
Eliza Orr
Ferdinand Sharp
Nastasia Wahlberg
Evelyn Yanez

Table of Contents

Acknowledgements

The supplemental math series *Math in a Cultural Context: Lessons Learned from Yup'ik Eskimo Elders* is based on traditional and present day wisdom and is dedicated to the late Mary George of Akiachak, Alaska. Mary contributed to every aspect of this long-term project, from her warm acceptance of people from all walks of life to her unique ideas and ways of putting together traditional Yup'ik knowledge with modern Western knowledge. Mary's contributions permeate this work. Without the dedication and perseverance of Mary and her husband, Frederick George, who tirelessly continues to work with this project, this work would not be possible. In particular, *Building a Fish Rack: Investigations into Proof, Properties, Perimeter, and Area* would not have been possible to develop without the assistance of many Yup'ik elders, community members, and teachers from Alaska: Joshua Phillip of Akiachak; Henry Alakayak and Jonah Lomack of Manokotak; and Arthur Jasper and Sam Ivan of Akiak. Years ago we built a fish rack together, studied it, and from these experiences laid the foundation for this module.

In addition, for the past twenty-two years Jerry Lipka has had the pleasure to work with and learn from Evelyn Yanez of Togiak, Alaska; Nancy and Ferdinand Sharp and Anecia and Jonah Lomack of Manokotak, Alaska; Linda Brown of Ekwok and Fairbanks, Alaska; Sassa Peterson of Homer, Alaska; and Margie Hastings of New Stuyahok, Alaska. Their contributions are immeasurable, as is their friendship. Our long-term relationships with elders who embraced this work wholeheartedly has made this difficult endeavor pleasurable as we each learn from each other. In particular, we would like to acknowledge Henry Alakayak of Manokotak, Alaska, who has been there for this project and has given unselfishly so that others could prosper from his knowledge; equally unselfishly contributing are Lilly and John Pauk of Manokotak, and Annie Blue, Mary Bavilla, Mary Active, and Emma Nanalook from Togiak—they came with stories that enriched us. Also Sam Ivan, Akiak, Joshua Phillip and George Moses of Akiachak, and Anuska Nanalook and Anecia and Mike Toyukak of Manokotak all provided knowledge about many aspects of traditional life, from Anecia's gifted storytelling and storyknifing to kayaks and other traditional Yup'ik crafts to countless stories about how to survive. We also thank George Charles for helping us to understand and for translating at meetings and Walkie Charles for his assistance in translating and understanding the various types of fish racks and for the humor he added to every meeting.

We would like to thank our dedicated staff, especially Flor Banks, whose highly refined organizational skills, determination to get the job done, and motivation to move this project forward from reading and editing manuscripts to holding the various pieces of this project together, has been an irreplaceable asset, and she has done it all with a smile. To Putt Clark, graphic artist extraordinaire, who kept up with every demand and produced more and better artwork than anyone could have hoped for and has worked with this project from the beginning to end-thank you. Thanks to Sandra Wildfeuer for writing the cultural and historical notes and assisting with the development of a number of the activities. Thanks to Sunna Fesler for her contributions of creative activities to this and other modules. We would like to thank Eliza and Ben Orr for producing the Yup'ik Glossary that accompanies this project and for all their hard work, Anna and Steve Jacobson for their linguistic work, and Nastasia Wahlberg for translating so many meetings over the years. We thank the University of Alaska Fairbanks student translators for their help in this module and others: Francisca Yanez, Ferdella Sharp, Lorrine Masterman, Roland White, Merna Lomack, Carolyn Hoover, Agnes Green, and Jamie Active.

We wish to acknowledge Kay Gilliland for her unflagging, hardworking dedication to this project. A special thanks to Leslie and Tom Dolan, Doug Noon, Janet Speed, Stacy Clark, and Jeff Jacobson for allowing us into their classrooms and for the wonderful ideas that they contributed to this project. To the Fairbanks North Star Borough School District, the Lower Yukon School District, the Yupiit School District, the St. Marys School District, the Anchorage School District, the Yukon Flats School District, and to the Southwest Region Schools for their cooperation in piloting modules. To all the other math writers, project and pilot teachers, and elders who have assisted this project.

To Roger Norris-Tull, dean of the School of Education, University of Alaska Fairbanks, who supported this work generously—thank you. Thanks to Sharon Nelson Barber, West Ed, for supporting this work in spirit and in action for more than a decade and to Guillermo (Willy) Solano-Flores, West Ed, for his assistance with assessments. We wish to thank Katherine Mulcrone for her hard work editing this module and Sue Mitchell for her final editing and page layout work.

Barbara L. Adams: I would like to give a special thanks to the Yup'ik elders, teachers, and consultants for accepting me into the project, filling me in on the details and history, inviting me into their homes and classrooms, and supporting me in their collaboration. I especially thank Nancy Sharp, Ferdinand Sharp, and Henry Alakayak of Manokotak and Evelyn Yanez of Togiak.

Thanks to the project staff, especially Jerry and Flor, for accepting me for who I am and what I can contribute. To my mother who taught me to be open-minded, my previous professors for providing me with a strong mathematical foundation, the people with the Interior-Aleutians Campus of UAF who introduced me to the remote ways of Alaska, and my friends who support my endeavors in this work—many thanks. Lastly to my husband, Todd, I thank you for your time, support, sacrifices, encouragement, and love.

Jerry Lipka: To my loving wife, Janet Schichnes, who supported me in countless ways that allowed me to complete this work. To my loving children, Alan and Leah, who shared me with so many other people. I appreciate all the wonderful time we spent and continue to spend together.

Although this has been a long-term collaborative endeavor, we hope that we have taken a small step to meet the desires of the elders for the next generation to be flexible thinkers, able to effectively function in the Yup'ik and Western worlds.

Introduction

Math in a Cultural Context

Lessons Learned from Yup'ik Eskimo Elders

Introduction to the Series

Math in a Cultural Context: Lessons Learned from Yup'ik Eskimo Elders[1] is a supplemental math curriculum based on the traditional wisdom and practices of the Yup'ik Eskimo people of southwest Alaska. The kindergarten to sixth-grade math modules that you are about to teach are the result of a decade-long collaboration between math educators, teachers, and Yup'ik Eskimo elders and teachers to connect cultural knowledge to school mathematics. To understand the rich environment from which this curriculum came, imagine traveling on a snowmachine over the frozen tundra and finding your way based on the position of the stars in the night sky. Or, in summer, paddling a sleek kayak across open waters shrouded in fog, yet knowing which way to travel toward land by the waves' pattern. Or imagine building a kayak or making clothing and accurately sizing them by visualizing or using body measures. This is a small sample of the activities in which modern Yup'ik people engage. The embedded mathematics formed the basis for this series of supplemental math modules. Each module is independent and lasts from three to eight weeks.

From 1999 through the spring of 2002, students who used these modules consistently outperformed students who used only their regular math textbooks, at statistically significant levels. This was true for both urban and rural students, both Caucasian and Alaska Native students. We believe that this supplemental curriculum will motivate your students and strengthen their mathematical understanding because of the engaging content, hands-on approach to problem-solving, and the emphasis on mathematical communication. Further, these modules build on students' everyday experiences and intuitive understandings, particularly in geometry, which is underrepresented in school.

The modules explore the everyday application of mathematics skills such as grouping, approximating, measuring, proportional thinking, informal geometry, and counting in base twenty and then presents these in terms of formal mathematics. Students move from the concrete and applied to more formal and abstract math. The activities are designed to meet the following goals:

- Students learn to solve mathematical problems that support an in-depth understanding of mathematical concepts.
- Students derive mathematical formulas and rules from concrete and practical applications.
- Students become flexible thinkers because they learn that there is more than one method of solving a mathematical problem.
- Students learn to communicate and think mathematically while they demonstrate their understanding to peers.
- Students learn content across the curriculum, since the lessons comprise Yup'ik Eskimo culture, literacy, geography, and science.

Beyond meeting some of the content (mathematics) and process standards of the National Council of Teachers of Mathematics (2000), the curriculum design and its activities respond to the needs of diverse learners. Many activities are designed for group work. One of the strategies for using group work is to provide leadership opportunities to students who may not typically be placed in that role. Also, the modules tap into a wide array of intellectual abilities—practical, creative, and analytic. We assessed modules that were tested in rural Alaska, urban Alaska, and suburban California, and found that students who were only peripherally involved in math became more active participants.

Students learn to reason mathematically by constructing models and analyzing practical tasks for their embedded mathematics. This enables them to generate and discover mathematical rules and formulas. In this way, we offer students a variety of ways to engage the math material through practical activity, spatial visual learning, analytic thinking, and creative thinking. They are constantly encouraged to communicate mathematically by presenting their understandings while other students are encouraged to provide alternate solutions, strategies, and counter arguments. This process also strengthens their deductive reasoning.

To summarize, the curriculum design includes strategies that engage students:
- cognitively, so that students use a variety of thinking strategies (analytic, creative, and practical);
- socially, so that students with different social, cognitive, and mathematical skills use those strengths to lead and help solve mathematical problems;
- pedagogically, so that students explore mathematical concepts and communicate and learn to reason mathematically by demonstrating their understanding of the concepts; and
- practically, as students apply or investigate mathematics to solve problems from their daily lives.

Pedagogical Approach Used in the Modules

The organization of the modules follows five distinctly different approaches to teaching and learning that converge into one system.

Expert-Apprentice Modeling

The first approach, expert-apprentice modeling, comes from Yup'ik elders and teachers and is supported by research in anthropology and education. Many lessons begin with the teacher (the expert) demonstrating a concept to the students (the apprentices). Following the theoretical position of the Russian psychologist Vygotsky (cited in Moll, 1990) and expert Yup'ik teachers (Lipka and Yanez, 1998) and elders, students begin to appropriate the knowledge of the expert (teacher), as the teacher and the more adept apprentices help other students learn. This establishes a collaborative classroom setting in which student-to-student and student-to-teacher dialogues are part of the classroom fabric.

Reform-Oriented Approach

The second pedagogical approach emphasizes student collaboration in solving "deeper" problems (Ma, 1999). This approach is supported by research in math classrooms and particularly by recent international studies (Stevenson et al., 1990; Stigler and Hiebert, 1998) that strongly suggest that math problems should be more in-depth and challenging and that students should understand the underlying principles, not merely use procedures competently. The modules present complex problems (two-step open-ended problems) that require students to think more deeply about mathematics.

Multiple Intelligences

Further, the modules tap into students' multiple intelligences. While some students may learn best from hands-on, real-world related problems, others may learn best when abstracting and deducing. This module provides opportunities to guide both modalities. Robert Sternberg's work (1997; 1998) influenced the development of these modules. He has consistently found that students who are taught so that they use their analytic, creative, and practical intelligences will outperform students who are taught using one modality, most often analytic. Thus, we have shaped our activities to engage students in this manner.

Mathematical Argumentation and Deriving Rules

The modules support a math classroom environment in which students explore the underlying mathematical rules as they solve problems. Through structured classroom communication, students will learn to work collaboratively in a problem-solving environment in which they learn to both appreciate alternative solutions strategies and evaluate these strategies and solutions. They present their mathematical solutions to their peers. Through discrepancies in strategies and solutions, students will communicate with and help each other to understand their reasoning and mathematical decisions. Mathematical discussions are encouraged to strengthen their mathematical and logical thinking as students share their findings. This requires classroom norms that support student communication, learning from errors, and viewing errors as an opportunity to learn rather than criticize. The materials in the modules (see Materials section) constrain the possibilities, guide students in a particular direction, and increase their chances of understanding the mathematical concepts. Students are given the opportunity to support their conceptual understanding by practicing it in the context of a particular problem.

Familiar and Unfamiliar Contexts Challenge Students' Thinking

By working in unfamiliar settings and facing new and challenging problems, students learn to think creatively. They gain confidence in their ability to solve both everyday problems and abstract mathematical questions, and their entire realm of knowledge and experience expands. Further, by making the familiar unfamiliar and by working on novel problems, students are encouraged to connect what they learn from one setting (everyday problems) with mathematics in another setting. For example, most sixth-grade students know about rectangles and how to calculate the area of a rectangle, but if you ask students to go outside and find the four corners of an eight-foot-by twelve-foot-rectangle without using rulers or similar instruments, they are faced with a challenging problem. As they work through this everyday application (which is needed to build any rectangular structure) and as they "prove" to their classmates that they do, in fact, have a rectangular base, they expand their knowledge of rectangles. In effect they must shift their thinking from considering rectangles as physical entities or as prototypical examples to understanding the salient properties of a rectangle. Similarly, everyday language, conceptions, and intuition may, in fact, be in the way of mathematical understanding and the precise meaning of mathematical terms. By treating familiar knowledge in unfamiliar ways, students explore and confront their own mathematical understandings and they begin to understand the world of mathematics.

These major principles guide the overall pedagogical approach to the modules.

The Organization of the Modules

The curriculum comprises twelve modules for kindergarten through sixth grade. Modules are divided into sections: activities, explorations, and exercises, with some variation between each module. Supplementary information is included in Cultural Notes, Teacher Notes, and Math Notes. Each module follows a particular cultural story line, and the mathematics connects directly to it. Some modules are designed around a children's story, and an illustrated text is included for the teacher to read to the class.

The module is a teacher's manual. It begins with a general overview of the activities ahead, an explanation of the math and pedagogy of the module, teaching suggestions, and a historical and cultural overview of the curriculum in general and of the specific module. Each activity includes a brief introductory statement, an estimated duration, goals, materials, any preclass preparatory instructions for the teacher, and the procedures for the class to carry out the activity. Assessments are placed at various stages, both intermittently and at the end of activities.

Illustrations help to enliven the text. Yup'ik stories and games are interspersed and enrich the mathematics. Overhead masters, worksheet masters, assessments, and suggestions for additional materials are attached at the end of each activity. An overhead projector is necessary. Blackline masters that can be made into overhead transparencies are an important visual enhancement of the activities, stories, and games. Supplemental aids—colored posters, coloring books, and CD-ROMs—are attached separately or may be purchased elsewhere. Such visual aids also help to further classroom discussion and understanding. CD-ROMs can be found at http://www.uaf.edu/educ/Grants/html/hp.html.

Resources and Materials Required to Teach the Modules

Materials

The materials and tools limit the range of mathematical possibilities, guiding students' explorations so that they focus upon the intended purpose of the lesson. For example, in the *Elastic Geometry* module, latex sheets are used to explore concepts of topology. Students can manipulate the latex to the degree necessary to discover the mathematics of the various activities and apply the rules of topology.

For materials and learning tools that are more difficult to find or that are directly related to unique aspects of this curriculum, we provide detailed instructions for the teacher and students on how to make those tools. For example, in *Going to Egg Island: Adventures in Grouping and Place Values,* students use a base-twenty abacus. Although the project has produced and makes available a few varieties of wooden abaci, detailed instructions are provided for the teacher and students on how to make a simple, inexpensive, and usable abacus with beads and pipe cleaners.

Each module and each activity lists all of the materials and learning tools necessary to carry it out. Some of the tools are expressly mathematical, such as interlocking centimeter cubes, abaci, and compasses. Others are particular to the given context of the problem, such as latex and black and white geometric pattern pieces. Many of the materials are items a teacher will probably have on hand, such as paper, markers, scissors, and rulers. Students learn to apply and manipulate the materials. The value of caring for the materials is underscored by the precepts of subsistence, which is based on processing raw materials and foods with maximum use and minimum waste. Periodically, we use food as part of an activity. In these instances, we encourage minimal waste.

Videos

To more vividly convey the knowledge of the elders that underlies the entire curriculum, we have produced a few videos to accompany some of the modules. For example, the *Going to Egg Island: Adventures in Grouping and Place Values* module includes videos of Yup'ik elders demonstrating some traditional Yup'ik games. We also have footage and recordings of the ancient chants that accompanied these games. The videos are available on CD-ROM and are readily accessible for classroom use.

Yup'ik Language Glossary and Math Terms Glossary

To help teachers and students get a better feel for the Yup'ik language, its sounds, and the Yup'ik words used to describe mathematical concepts in this curriculum, we have developed a Yup'ik glossary on CD-ROM. Each word is recorded in digital form and can be played back in Yup'ik. The context of the word is provided, giving teachers and students a better sense of the Yup'ik concept, not just its Western "equivalent." Pictures and illustrations often accompany the word for additional clarification.

Values

There are many important Yup'ik values associated with each module. The elders counsel against waste; they value listening, learning, working hard, being cooperative, and passing knowledge on to others. These values are expressed in the contents of the Yup'ik stories that accompany the modules, in the cultural notes, and in various activities. Similarly, Yup'ik people as well as other traditional people continue to produce, build, and make crafts from raw materials. Students who engage in these modules also learn how to make simple mathematical tools fashioned around such themes as Yup'ik border patterns and building model kayaks, fish racks, and smokehouses. Students learn to appreciate and value other cultures.

Cultural Notes

Most of the mathematics used in the curriculum comes from our direct association and long-term collaboration with Yup'ik Eskimo elders and teachers. We have included many cultural notes to more fully describe and explain the purposes, origins, and variations associated with a particular traditional activity. Each module is based on a cultural activity and follows a Yup'ik cultural storyline, along which the activities and lessons unfold. The activities reflect the various aspects or stages of the particular activity.

Math Notes

We want to ensure that teachers who may want to teach these materials but feel unsure of some of the mathematical concepts will feel supported by the math notes. These provide background material to help teachers better understand the mathematical concepts presented in the activities and exercises of each module. For example, in the *Perimeter and Area* module, the math notes give a detailed description of a rectangle and describe the geometric proofs one would apply to ascertain whether or not a shape is a rectangle. The *Rectangular Prism* module explores the geometry of three-dimensional objects, and the math notes include information on the geometry of rectangular prisms, including proofs, to facilitate the instructional process. In every module, connections are made between the "formal math," its practical application, and the classroom strategies for teaching the math.

Teacher Notes

The main function of the teacher notes is to bring awareness to the key pedagogical aspects of the lesson. For example, they provide suggestions on how to facilitate students' mathematical understanding through classroom organization strategies, classroom communication, and ways of structuring lessons. Teacher Notes also make suggestions for ways of connecting out-of-school knowledge with schooling.

Assessment

Assessment and instruction are interrelated throughout the modules. Assessments are embedded within instructional activities, and teachers are encouraged to carefully observe, listen, and challenge their students' thinking. We call this active assessment, which allows teachers to assess how well students have learned to solve the mathematical and cultural problems introduced in a module.

Careful attention has been given to developing assessment techniques and tools that evaluate both the conceptual and procedural knowledge of students. We agree with Ma (1999) that having one type of knowledge without the other, or a lack of understanding of the link between the two, will produce only partial understanding. The goal here is to produce relational understanding in mathematics. Instruction and assessment have been developed and aligned to ensure that both types of knowledge are acquired, and this has been accomplished using both traditional and alternative techniques.

The specific details and techniques for assessment when applicable are included within activities. The three main tools for collecting and using assessment data follow.

Journals

Each student can keep a journal for daily entries, consisting primarily of responses to specific activities. Student journals serve as a current record of their work and a long-term record of their increasing mathematical knowledge and ability to communicate this knowledge. Many of the modules and their activities require students to predict, sketch, define, explain, calculate, design, and solve problems. Often, students will be asked to revisit their responses after a series of activities, so that they can appreciate and review what they have learned. Student journals also provide the teacher with insight into their thinking, making it an active tool in the assessment and instructional process.

Observation

Observing and listening to their students lets teachers learn about the strategies that students use to analyze and solve various problems. Listening to informal conversations between students as they work cooperatively on problems provides further insight into their strategies. Through observation, teachers also learn about their students' attitudes toward mathematics and their skills in cooperating with others. Observation is an excellent way to link assessment with instruction.

Adaptive Instruction

The goal of the summary assessment in this curriculum is to adapt instruction to the skills and knowledge needed by a group of students. From reviewing journal notes to simply observing, teachers learn which mathematical processes their students are able to effectively use and which ones they need to practice more. Adaptive assessment and instruction complete the link between assessment and instruction.

An Introduction to the Land and Its People, Geography, and Climate

Flying over the largely uninhabited expanse of southwest Alaska on a dark winter morning, one looks down at a white landscape interspersed with trees, winding rivers, rolling hills, and mountains. One sees a handful of lights sprinkled here, a handful there. Half of Alaska's 600,000-plus population lives in Anchorage. The other half is dispersed among smaller cities such as Fairbanks and Juneau and among the over two hundred rural villages that are scattered across the state. Landing on the village airstrip, which is usually gravel and, in the winter, covered with smooth, hard-packed snow, one is taken to the village by either car or snowmachine. Hardly any villages or regional centers are connected to a road system. The major means of transportation between these communities is by small plane, boat, and snowmachine, depending on the season.

It is common for the school to be centrally located. Village roads are usually unpaved, and people drive cars, four wheelers, and snowmachines. Houses are typically made from modern materials and have electricity and running water. Over the past twenty years, Alaska villages have undergone major changes, both technologically and culturally. Most now have television, a full phone system, modern water and sewage treatment facilities, an airport, and a small store. Some also have a restaurant, and a few even have a small hotel and taxicab service. Access to medical care and public safety are still sporadic, with the former usually provided by a local health care worker and a community health clinic, or by health care workers from larger cities or regional centers who visit on a regular basis. Serious medical emergencies require air evacuation to either Anchorage or Fairbanks.

The Schools

Years of work have gone into making education as accessible as possible to rural communities. Almost every village has an elementary school, and most have a high school. Some also have a higher education satellite facility, computer access to higher education courses, or options that enable students to work on and earn college credits while in their respective home communities. Vocational education is taught in some of the high schools, and there are also special vocational education facilities in some villages. While English has become the dominant language throughout Alaska, many Yup'ik children in the villages of this region still learn Yup'ik at home.

Yup'ik Village Life Today

Most villagers continue to participate in the seasonal rounds of hunting, fishing, and gathering. Although many modern conveniences are located within the village, when one steps outside of its narrow bounds, one is immediately aware of one's vulnerability in this immense and unforgiving land, where one misstep can lead to disaster. Depending upon their location (coastal community, riverine, or interior), villagers hunt and gather the surrounding resources. These include sea mammals, fish, caribou, and many types of berries. The seasonal subsistence calendar illustrates which activities take place during the year (see Fig. 1). Knowledgeable elders know how to cross rivers and find their way through ice fields, navigating the seemingly featureless tundra by using directional indicators such as frozen grass and the constellations in the night sky. All of this can mean the difference between life and death. In the summer, when this largely treeless plain covered with moss and grass thaws into a large swamp dotted with small lakes, the consequences of ignorance, carelessness, and inexperience can be just as devastating. Underwater hazards in the river, such as submerged logs, can capsize a boat, dumping the occupants into the cold, swift current. Overland travel is much more difficult during the warm months due to the marshy ground and many waterways, and one can easily become disoriented and get lost. The sea is also integral to life in this region and requires its own set of skills and specialized knowledge to be safely navigated.

The Importance of the Land: Hunting and Gathering

Basic subsistence skills include knowing how to read the sky to determine the weather and make appropriate travel plans, being able to read the land to find one's way, knowing how to build an emergency shelter and, in the greater scheme, how to hunt and gather food and properly process and store it. In addition, the byproducts of subsistence activities, such as carved walrus tusks, pelts and skins made into clothing or decorative items, and a variety of other utilitarian and arts and crafts products provide an important source of cash for many rural residents.

Hunting and gathering are still of great importance in modern Yup'ik society. A young man's first seal hunt is celebrated; family members who normally live and work in one of the larger cities will often fly home to help when the salmon are running; whole families still gather to go berry picking. The importance of hunting and gathering in daily life is further reflected in the legislative priorities expressed by rural residents in Alaska. These focus on such things as subsistence hunting regulations, fishing quotas, and resource development and environmental issues that affect the well-being of game animals and subsistence vegetation.

Conclusion

We developed this curriculum in a Yup'ik context. The traditional subsistence and other skills of the Yup'ik people incorporate spatial, geometrical, and proportional reasoning and other mathematical reasoning. We have attempted to offer you and your students a new way to approach and apply mathematics while also learning about Yup'ik culture. Our goal has been to present math as practical information that is inherent in everything we do. We hope your students will adopt and incorporate some of this knowledge and add it to their learning base.

We hope you and your students will benefit from the mathematics, culture, geography, and literature embedded in *Math in a Cultural Context: Lessons Learned from Yup'ik Eskimo Elders*. The elders who guided this work emphasized that the next generation of children should be flexible thinkers and leaders. In a small way, we hope that this curriculum guides you and your students along this path.

Tua-ii ingrutuq [This is not the end].

References

Lipka, Jerry, and Evelyn Yanez. 1998. "Identifying and Understanding Cultural Differences: Toward Culturally Based Pedagogy." In *Transforming the Culture of Schools,* edited by Lipka, J., Mohatt, G., and the Ciulistet, 111–137. Mahwah, NJ: Lawrence Erlbaum.

Ma, Liping. 1999. *Knowing and Teaching Elementary Mathematics*. Mahwah, NJ: Lawrence Erlbaum.

Moll, Luis. 1990. *Vygotsky and Education: Instructional Implications and Applications of Sociohistorical Psychology*. Cambridge: Cambridge University Press.

National Council of Teachers of Mathematics. 2000. *Principles and Standards for School Mathematics*. Reston, VA: National Council of Teachers of Mathematics.

Sternberg, Robert. 1997. *Successful Intelligence*. New York: Plume.

Sternberg, Robert. 1998. Principles of Teaching for Successful Intelligence. *Educational Psychologist 33*, 65–72.

Stevenson, Harold, Max Lummis, Shin-Yin Lee, and James Stigler. 1990. *Making the Grade in Mathematics*. Arlington, VA: National Council of Teachers of Mathematics.

Stigler, James, and James Hiebert. 1998. Teaching is a Cultural Activity. *American Educator* 22(4):4–11.

Notes

1. This math series is based on *Adapting Yup'ik Elders' Knowledge: Pre-K-to-6 Math and Instructional Materials Development,* a project sponsored by the National Science Foundation (NSF), award #9618099.

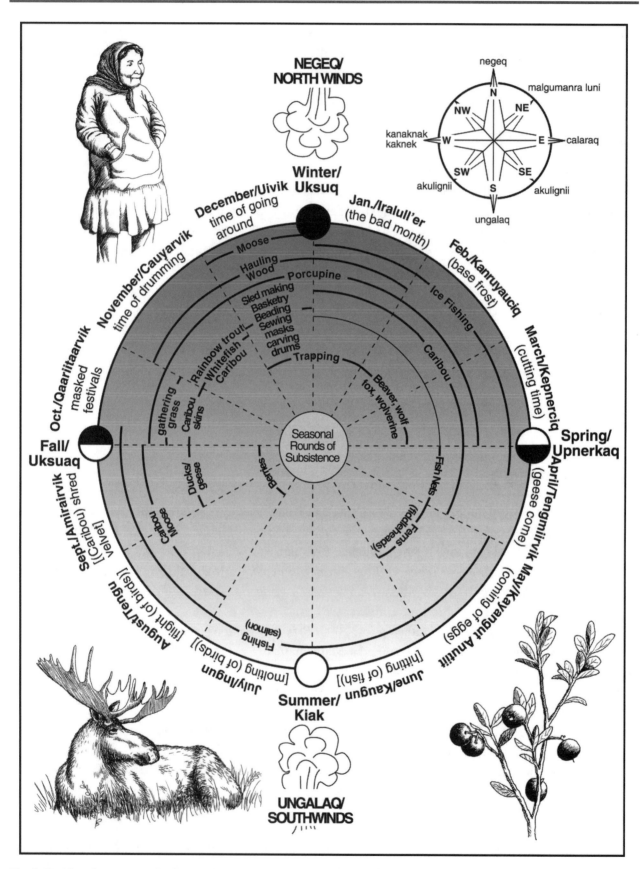

Fig. 1: Yearly subsistence calendar

Introduction

Building a Fish Rack:
Investigations into Proof, Properties, Perimeter, and Area

Math Summary

The hands-on activities related to building a fish rack for the harvest of salmon form the basis upon which formal mathematics develops in this module. Students engage in activities that simulate the way Yup'ik elders might go about designing and building a fish rack for drying salmon. In the process, they consider a number of factors: ease of access, durability, strength, and capacity to hold a large amount of fish. For example, students in one activity learn to maximize the area of a rectangular drying rack, given a fixed perimeter. This exercise applies directly to the real-life situation in which materials such as wood are often limited, and Yup'ik fishermen thus optimize the drying rack with the few resources they have. In many exercises students increase their understanding of both Yup'ik culture and Western mathematics by learning cultural constructs, such as *sufficient* and *adequate* instead of *maximum* and *best*.

Building a Fish Rack: Investigations into Proof, Properties, Perimeter, and Area provides opportunities to pursue open-ended problems and extended problem-solving projects. For example, students begin with the overall problem of how to construct a model of a fish rack. From there, they explore a wealth of associated problems such as determining the area for a variety of shapes and determining the type of three-dimensional shape that is most structurally stable. This large investigation allows students to formulate questions, engage in hands-on learning, and represent their solutions verbally, numerically, graphically, geometrically, and symbolically. Mathematical communication is emphasized in this module as students talk and listen within their groups and with the rest of the class about the progress of their project, and as they write and draw in their journals.

Students use spatial reasoning and proportional reasoning. For example, in Activity 12, they investigate the relationship between perimeter and area when the perimeter is held constant. In Activity 16, when designing the support structures for the fish racks, students explore the relationship between shape and strength, and shape and stability.

Students apply the mathematics they are learning to new situations. For instance, they use their knowledge of the formula for the area of a rectangle to determine the formula for the area of a trapezoid. In another exercise, they apply their newly learned tasks of conjecturing and proving to discover properties of other quadrilaterals based on known properties of rectangles.

Proof

Proof is a fundamental concept usually associated with geometry. However, proof is also embedded in other mathematical fields. In fact, even in early elementary schooling, young children while performing simple arithmetic operations are using a process of proof. For example, $2 + 3 = 5$. Students know and can show the validity of this statement through counting. This is a proof.

In this module, we use a concrete hands-on approach that allows the concept of proof to be accessible at an earlier age than normal. This approach to proof will not only prepare students for geometry in high school, but concurrently provides students with a stance to think of math meaningfully, rather than as mere manipulation.

In this module, often students are asked to prove concepts around shape. For example, students will consider if a rectangle has diagonals of equal lengths. To best formulate how to go about this problem, students are asked to make a conjecture (a guess showing the direction and the truth of the statement), provide proof through words, drawings, physical evidence, or counter examples, and then state the conclusion. One conjecture for this example would be if an object is a rectangle then its diagonals have the same length. Another conjecture would be if an object is a rectangle then its diagonals do not have the same length. In both cases, a direction is stated (start with a rectangular object and prove a statement about the length of its diagonals), and a truth is imposed (the diagonals are or are not the same length). When going about the proof, since the object is known to be a rectangle, any properties of the rectangle can be used. Once students show that the lengths of the diagonals must be the same if they started with a rectangle, then the conclusion is that all rectangles have diagonals with equal length despite the original conjecture.

Many important ideas are embodied in the example above such as the direction of proof, the need to show the property holds all the time, and the idea of using a counter example. Another key concept is that proof forces properties to match the definition. This may be harder to see depending on how far removed the properties are from the definition of the object. In the case above, the diagonals are not used to define the property of a rectangle, although from equal diagonals the properties of a rectangle, such as opposite sides of equal lengths and parallel and all angles 90 degrees, can be determined. To further understand this point, consider a related conjecture with a different direction.

Conjecture: If the lengths of the diagonals of a four-sided object are the same, then the four-sided object is a rectangle. In this example, the conjecture is not the same as the one stated in the previous paragraph. The starting point now becomes an unknown four-sided object with diagonals of the same length, and so the shape is unknown and properties of a rectangle in particular can not be used. When working through the proof, students may be able to show that starting here they can indeed construct a rectangle. However, other students may be able to show that a trapezoid can also be constructed with that same starting point. The conclusion may then be that this conjecture is not always true or that it is false as shown by the counter example of the trapezoid. This gets at the idea that to prove something mathematically means to prove that it will always be true, not just sometimes true.

Procedures for Teaching Problem-Solving

Outlined in the following two sections entitled "Teacher Modeling" and "Students Take Leadership Roles," are some problem-solving strategies. We devised these strategies based on the work of three educators. Polya (1957) formulated such problem-solving questions as "What is the unknown?"; "What is the data?"; "What is the condition?"; "Do you know a related problem?" Sternberg (2001) gave us insights into student learning by suggesting that students learn more about any subject if they use creative, analytic and practical intelligences in the learning process. Brady (1990) introduced us to an instructional strategy, reciprocal teaching, used in reading instruction but easily adapted to mathematics. Reciprocal teaching allows students to work in small groups, taking turns assuming the role of teacher. The ideas presented by Polya, Sternberg and Brady are consistent with our work in collaboration with Yup'ik teachers (Lipka, 1998) which also supports group-oriented, expert-apprentice modeling in which students learn to utilize the skills and knowledge of more expert learners.

As you follow the suggested problem-solving techniques throughout the course of the module, you will want to encourage and aid students in establishing problem-solving norms in their groups, generating multiple solutions through diverse approaches, justifying results and correctness mathematically both within groups and amongst groups, and reconciling differences in approaches and solutions. While students work in groups, you will want to encourage students to visit other groups, reach conclusions within their own group, and talk among groups. Then challenge them to create an entire class conclusion by discussing, sharing, showing, and presenting group results to the entire class.

An assessment tool grows naturally out of the suggested problem-solving techniques. At first, students may say, "I don't know" when asked to solve a problem. Note such comments, the date, the problem, and other relevant information. As the course proceeds, note what students continue to say and do as they solve novel problems. As students move from "I don't know" and use of "trial and error" to develop more effective problem-solving skills, your documentation will help you to assist the students in becoming more independent learners throughout the remainder of the module.

Sample Problem

This problem is adapted from George Lenchner's (1983) *Creative Problem Solving in School Mathematics*.

Example

Two king salmon weigh the same as two chum and six red salmon. A chum weighs the same as three red salmon. How much does a king weigh in terms of a red salmon?

Solution

Two king weigh the same as 2 chum and 6 red salmon, so $2k = 2c + 6r$.

A chum weighs the same as 3 red salmon, so $c = 3r$.

Therefore, $2k = 2(3r) + 6r$, $2k = 6r + 6r$, $2k = 12r$, $k = 6r$.

A king weighs the same as 6 red salmon.

Modeling and Talking Aloud: A Sample Script

This approach is similar to the "Read Aloud—Think Aloud" approach used in content reading (Vacca and Vacca, 1999).

First approach: Here is a verbatim account of how one of the writers solved this problem:

I am trying to understand what the problem is saying. I was confused by the language—"2 king weigh the same as 2 chum and 6 reds." So then I said to myself that two kings equal 2 chums and a chum weighs the same as 3 red salmon. Then, logic tells me that two kings can't be the same as 2 chums. Something is wrong here.

Drawing a picture looks like a lot of work and it might not be a good strategy here. My first reaction to this problem is to write it out as a symbol. I realized that kings, chums, and reds are the important things. So, I used symbols for them instead, k = kings, c = chums, and r = reds. This looks very straightforward when you work it out; the chum weighs the same as 3 red salmon. Instead of using chums I will use 3 reds. The reason for this is that a chum is the same as 3 reds. Why did I solve the problem this way? There is too much information—because the first sentence has three different types of salmon.

Three variables make it too hard to compare. So, I use the other information to make that comparison easier. That is where we get 2k = 12r. From here the problem is easier to understand and solve. We can see that 1k has to be equal to 6r.

Second approach: Another approach is to use manipulatives to act out the problem. Be sure to talk through the problem-solving as you did in the first approach.

For example, use a banana to represent a king, an apple for a chum, and a cherry for the red (Fig. 2). Put two bananas in a bowl to show the first group. Put two apples with 6 cherries in another bowl to show the second group. Since the other sentence in the problem says a chum is the same as three reds, replace each set of three cherries with an apple. Now, the problem is simplified because there are only bananas and apples (or kings and chum) left.

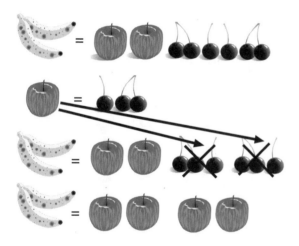

Fig. 2: Using manipulatives to think out the problem

Problem-Solving Approach

I. Teacher Modeling

For the first phase of the problem-solving strategies, the teacher models for the students what to do, as in the sample problem/solution strategies previously shown. The teacher explains the pedagogical technique at the outset of the demonstration so the students know what's happening in the first "definition" phase. Choosing a problem in the module (or constructing his/her own problem), the teacher should follow these steps.

Problem Definition

- Read the problem aloud.

- Go through the vocabulary. Do we know what the words mean?

- If not, can we infer the meaning of the unknown word(s) from the rest of the problem?

- Ask: Do we understand the problem?

- Ask: What type of problem is this? An addition problem or subtraction with fractions? Etc.

- Ask: What information is given?

- Ask: What information is missing? What do we need to find out?

Pedagogical Technique

The teacher should explain that sometimes it helps to understand a problem by explaining it to someone else or by rewriting the problem in your own words.

Devise a Plan

The teacher demonstrates how to devise a plan by asking, "What can we do to solve this problem?" We can

- make a table.

- find a pattern.

- solve a simpler problem.

- use logic.

- apply trial and error.

- create an experiment.

- draw a picture.

- ask students for other possibilities.

Carry Out the Plan

The teacher demonstrates how to carry out the plan. This step may include using paper and pencil and making the necessary calculations. The teacher should emphasize that if a problem-solver (including the teacher) gets stuck before finding an answer, she/he may need to throw away the first plan and devise a new one.

Looking Back

The teacher emphasizes that the last step is to review the question and decide if she/he answered it correctly. The teacher demonstrates methods of reviewing the problem and solution.

II. Students Take Leadership Roles

The second phase involves students working in small groups (two to five students per group) and taking on the role of the teacher. It is important for students to shift roles so everyone can have a turn taking the lead in prompting the other members of the group to use the problem-solving strategies. Every member of the group should independently, with discussion, carry out the plan. Have students take on the following roles:

• Leader—this person leads the discussion within the group to help identify with what type of problem they are working.

• Planner—once the problem is established, a student other than the leader in the group now takes on the role of facilitating the planning.

• Evaluator—after the students have carried out the plan, this student checks or facilitates the process of checking whether the result satisfies the requirements of the problem.

Students change and rotate roles for each new problem-solving session. Encourage groups of students to visit other groups to view and discuss different approaches.

Mathematical Modeling

The process of mathematical modeling involves fitting a real-world situation into a mathematical framework and thus connects culture to math. Modeling often requires knowledge of many areas of mathematics and is not usually a simple task since mathematics assumes an ideal world. Often, once a mathematical model is built, it is continually revisited and revised since a model can never be perfect.

Just as fish rack designs differ across Alaska based upon years of experience building them and using them, any mathematical model of a fish rack should incorporate the same knowledge. In particular, climatic conditions, local resources, geographic locations and cultural conditions have aided in the evolution of fish racks over long periods of time. When building a mathematical model of a fish rack students will start with an idealized version and then introduce these variables to make it more realistic.

Students progress from the properties and purposes of the fish rack to viewing the fish rack as a group of mathematical objects. As students develop their modeling skills they investigate various measurements, specifically perimeter and area, and concepts of strength and stability related to those shapes. The mathematical modeling culminates with students building model fish racks based on the collection of cultural, physical, and mathematical information obtained through the activities.

The fish rack models built by the students can be revisited and refined by using the sixth-grade companion modules in the series. In each of the other modules students have a glimpse at other important attributes, such as the size and weight of each fish, the need for drying the fish, and the smoking process to preserve the fish which will allow them to improve on the mathematical models they started in this module.

NCTM Standards and This Module

The skills and knowledge emphasized in these activities relate directly to the NCTM standards. The specific NCTM standards addressed by this module are listed here. Aspects of grades 6–8 math content included in this module focus on problem-solving, reasoning and proof, communication and connections. Further description and examples of each standard can be found at the NCTM website: http://standards.nctm.org/document/chapter6/index.htm.

Standard 2: Algebra

- Use mathematical models to represent and understand quantitative relationships

- Analyze change in various contexts

Standard 3: Geometry

- Analyze characteristics and properties of two-and three-dimensional geometric shapes and develop mathematical arguments about geometric relationships

- Specify locations and describe spatial relationships using coordinate geometry and other representational systems

- Use visualization, spatial reasoning and geometric modeling to solve problems

Standard 4: Measurement

- Understand measurable attributes of objects and the units, systems, and processes of measurement

- Apply appropriate techniques, tools, and formulas to determine measurements

Standard 6: Problem Solving

- Build new mathematical knowledge through problem-solving

- Solve problems that arise in mathematics and in other contexts

- Apply and adapt a variety of appropriate strategies to solve problems

- Monitor and reflect on the process of mathematical problem-solving

Standard 7: Reasoning & Proof

- Recognize reasoning and proof as fundamental aspects of mathematics

- Make and investigate mathematical conjectures

- Develop and evaluate mathematical arguments and proofs

- Select and use various types of reasoning and methods of proof

Standard 8: Communication

- Organize and consolidate their mathematical thinking through communication
- Communicate their mathematical thinking coherently and clearly to peers, teachers, and others
- Analyze and evaluate the mathematical thinking and strategies of others
- Use the language of mathematics to express mathematical ideas precisely

Standard 9: Connections

- Recognize and use connections among mathematical ideas
- Understand how mathematical ideas interconnect and build on one another to produce a coherent whole
- Recognize and apply mathematics in contexts outside of mathematics

Standard 10: Representations

- Create and use representations to organize, record, and communicate mathematical ideas
- Select, apply, and translate among mathematical representations to solve problems
- Use representations to model and interpret physical, social, and mathematical phenomena

History of Alaska Fisheries

Since the 1880s, the commercial salmon fishery has comprised an important part of Alaska's economy. Bristol Bay in southwest Alaska has the largest red salmon fishery in the world and is one of the many bountiful salmon fishing areas in Alaska. It remains Alaska's hub for both subsistence and commercial salmon fishing.

Starting in 1904, Bristol Bay's treacherous waters could only be commercially fished using double-ender sailboats, which were a little over 29 feet (8.8 m) long. These were owned by the canneries, and fishermen used them for free but had to maintain them. The sailboats were not as efficient or easy to use as motorboats, and no one is sure why they were the only fishing boats allowed for so many years. Perhaps it was to avoid overfishing, or because fishermen were easier and cheaper to replace than expensive outboard motors. In 1951, the law changed and the sailboats were abandoned in favor of motorboats. Photos of an early twentieth-century fishery and a present-day fishery (Figs. 3 and 4) are included courtesy of the Rasmusen Library, University of Alaska Fairbanks.

With some of the highest tide fluctuations in the world, where the differences are often as much as 20 feet (6.1 m) or more, Bristol Bay challenges even the best boat navigation under ideal weather conditions. Relying exclusively on a sail required strength, courage, endurance and experience. Many a boat was stranded on a sandbar in the ebb, or washed over in the incoming flow. Combined with the violent and frequent storms of the area, a 2,000 to 3,000 pound (907 to 1,361 kg) load of salmon in the boat, cold water, a tired crew and a minimum of safety precautions and gear, the recipe for a dangerous occupation was complete. Many fishermen were swept overboard; others drowned when their boats capsized. While they tried to help each other, the wind and waves often made it impossible to rescue people from the rough water. Even for the hardiest crew with the most experience, making it through another fishing season was often a matter of luck.

Many Yup'ik participate in Bristol Bay's commercial fishery, selling their salmon to local canneries and processors. Others fish only to meet their subsistence needs, catching and drying enough salmon to feed their families over the long winter. Some people participate in both commercial and subsistence fisheries.

Fig. 3: Nushagak salmon fishery of the early twentieth century   *Fig. 4: Present-day fishery, Bristol Bay*

Cultural Note: Killer Weather

It blew harder and harder, until it was shrieking at 60 mph [97 km/hr]. Great breakers and rollers tossed in the main channel. We knew that the tide, pushed by the wind, would come in swiftly and that our boat could easily swamp. "We'll have to work fast, Al," Joe (his partner) warned.

We took the 25-foot [7.6 m] mast down and lashed it across the gunnels so that it stuck out seven or eight feet [2.1 to 2.4 m] on each side, hoping it would prevent the boat from rolling when the first wall of water struck. We buried our two anchors so that they and the boat formed a "Y" and waited. I wasn't cold, but I shivered as the southeaster moaned, and as we watched the frothing seas in the nearby channel.

A wall of water rushed across the flat as the tide rose. The boat lifted and bounced against the bottom as the wave receded.... By the third bump we were afloat.... And then we were pitching among the waves, riding at anchor.... The anchors held as the water deepened. When there was five feet [1.5 m] under us we hoisted sail, cut the line to one anchor, and pulled the other. With reduced sail we fought our way ten miles [16 km] to the Gravel Spit, but the wind was so strong that it cracked our mast. We dropped anchor to wait for a Monkey Boat—one of the power boats used for towing sailboats to and from fishing grounds.

Eight fishermen drowned that night. I watched two of them die.... As we clung to the boat, watching and hoping for a Monkey Boat, PAF (Pacific American Fisheries) sailboat No. 5, upside down, drifted near. Her crew of two clung to the bottom.

Except for the centerboard hold, there were no handholds for them—it was like trying to hang onto a whale's back. As the capsized boat pitched and rolled, the center-board floated up and down, making hamburger out of fingers in the centerboard hole; even, perhaps, actually cutting fingers off.

The boat was so near I thought I could push our 30-foot [9.1 m] sprit close enough so one of the fishermen could grab it. But it wasn't to be. There was nothing else we could do. They drifted off and both soon slid from the hull and disappeared into the stormy seas.

"Make some coffee," Joe gruffly ordered, his face a mask. I was young then, and I thought Joe was callous. He wasn't.... We had all we could do to save ourselves, and Joe knew it if I didn't. The scalding coffee helped. (Andree, 1986.)

Fig. 5: Bristol Bay "double-ender" used for fishing until 1951

The Fish

Salmon have constituted a vital traditional food source for Alaska Natives for over 10,000 years. They are also key to the bay and riverine ecology, feeding whales, bears, seals, otters, and other species of fish. Other important fish include herring, halibut, black fish, bull heads, grayling, pike, smelt, trout, arctic char and white fish.

Salmon are a migratory species of fish, meaning they travel from one feeding ground to another. The largest migration for these fish is from freshwater to saltwater, and then back to freshwater. This outmigration from freshwater to the marine environment takes place in spring and early summer. Depending on the species, salmon may travel just a few miles from their freshwater spawning grounds to the ocean, as for example some pinks do. Others travel much further. For example, a Yukon king salmon may travel 2,300 miles (3,700 km) as a smolt to reach the ocean, where it will range widely in the North Pacific and Bering Sea, sometimes as far away as Japan. After at least two years of feeding in saltwater, it will swim back up the Yukon some 2,300 miles (3,700 km) into Canada, and return to its birth stream to spawn. This journey home takes place over a period of approximately sixty days.

Alaska's Salmon

Because the Alaska coast meets the Pacific Ocean, all five species of Pacific salmon are found in Alaska's waters.

Pink or *humpback* salmon are the most numerous. They normally weigh between 3.5 and 4 pounds (1.6 to 1.8 kg) and average some 20 to 25 inches (51 to 64 cm) in length. As adults, they are a bright, steely blue on top and their sides are a silvery color. Many large, black spots are scattered on their back and entire tail fin. Their scales are small and their flesh is pink.

During spawning, all Pacific salmon undergo a remarkable metamorphosis. Their color changes, and the males develop hooked jaws, often with teeth, and a prominent hump on their back. Pink male salmon change to brown or black on top and have a white belly. The females turn olive green with dusky bars or patches on top and a light-colored belly.

Fig. 6: Pink salmon before the change

Sockeye, also called *red* because of the color of their meat, are the second most abundant salmon in Alaska. The adults are long and slender, a little larger than the pinks, with a metallic green-blue color on the back and top of the head, iridescent silver on the sides, and white or silver on the belly. Fine, black speckles might be sprinkled over the back. During spawning, males develop the characteristic humped back and hooked jaws, and sharp teeth called *kype*. Both males and females turn brilliant to dark red on their backs and sides, pale to olive green on their heads and upper jaws, and white on their lower jaws.

Fig. 7: Pink female after the change

Fig. 8: Pink male after the change

Fig. 9: Coho salmon before the change

Fig. 10: Coho salmon female after the change

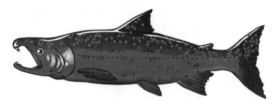

Fig. 11: Coho salmon male after the change

Chum or *dog* salmon are the third most numerous. The adults are a metallic greenish-blue on top with fine, black speckles and are about the same in size as the red salmon. During spawning their color changes to include vertical green and purple bars. The females develop a dark, horizontal band along the lateral line and faint green and purple vertical bars.

Coho or *silver* salmon are the fourth most numerous. Adults weigh between 8 and 12 pounds (3.6 to 5.4 kg) and are 24 to 30 inches (61 to 76 cm) long. They are a bright silver color, with small black spots on the back and on the upper lobe of the tail fin. During spawning, both males and females develop dark heads and backs and maroon to reddish sides.

Chinook or *king* salmon are the largest in size but the least abundant salmon in Alaska. They weigh anywhere from 4 to over 50 pounds (1.8 to 22.7 kg), depending on their age. Adults are a bluish-green color on the back, silvery on the sides and white on the belly. They have black, irregular spotting on the back and dorsal fins and on both lobes of the tail fin. They also have a black coloring along the gum line. During spawning, their color ranges from red to copper to almost black, depending on the age of the fish and its location. Males have a deeper color than females.

Salmon Life Cycle

While each of the five salmon species named above has its own particular migratory patterns and spawning habits, there are similarities among them. Pacific salmon are born in freshwater lakes or streams, where they spend up to two years growing. Then they travel to the ocean, where they feed and grow for an additional one to four years, depending on the species. When they reach adulthood, they return to freshwater to spawn. The type of freshwater in which they spawn varies. For example, some pink salmon may spawn within a few miles of the coast, chum spawn in the small side channels of large rivers, and chinook spawn in relatively deep and moving river water.

Pacific salmon usually return to their place of birth to spawn the next generation of fish, but how they find their way back to this precise creek remains somewhat of a mystery. Some evidence indicates that they may be using the magnetic forces of the earth, which they perceive through the lateral markings on their body. Some scientists believe that sockeye might use the position of the sun and the moon, and the Earth's magnetic field to guide them both to the ocean and back to fresh water. Salmon are also sensitive to electrical currents in the water, particularly for hunting, and perhaps also for guidance. Other evidence points to their sense of smell. King and coho salmon seem to have an especially strong *homing instinct*.

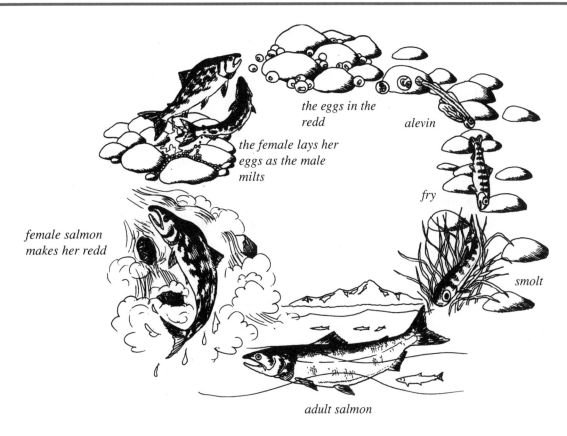

Fig. 12: Salmon life cycle

Spawning Process

Once the adults arrive at their stream, they begin the spawning process. The female digs a nest, or *redd*, in the gravel with her tail and deposits the eggs in it. The number of eggs released can vary from 1,500 to 4,500, depending on the species. As the eggs are released, the male swims over them and releases *milt* to fertilize them. Using her tail, the female covers the eggs with gravel. Laying the eggs and fertilizing them is called *spawning*, and within one or two weeks after the adults spawn, they die.

Stage of Development	Numbers of Surviving Fish
Egg to Fry	2430
Fry to Smolt	1860
Smolt to Adult	57

Fig. 13: Red salmon survival statistics when farm salmon are released into the water as smolt starting with a total of 3,000 eggs released

The eggs hatch within 90 to 120 days, usually in early spring. When the young emerge, the egg sac is still attached and provides nourishment. At this stage, the young are called *alevin*, and remain in the gravel. They live here until May or June, when they leave the gravel and enter the stream as *fry*. Depending on the species, they will feed as fry for up to two years, then travel to the ocean for further feeding. At this stage they are called *smolt*. In Alaska, they will end up in the Pacific Ocean or the Bering Sea. They spend the next two to five years or even more living and feeding in the ocean as adult salmon.

From the time they exist as eggs, predators are a constant threat to salmon. This is part of the salmon's important role in the complex ecological web of its environment. Birds and larger fish eat the eggs and the fry. In the ocean, they nourish many other species: beluga whales, sea lions, seals, salmon sharks and sea otters. Commercial, sport and subsistence fishermen also depend on the salmon for their commercial and nutritional survival.

Fig. 14: Beluga Whale: a major predator of salmon

The Salmon Run

The salmon migration home to produce the next generation of fish is called the *salmon run*. Every summer through early fall, at a fairly regular time, a new group of salmon "runs" home. Along the Kuskokwim River, the kings usually begin running by the first of June and continue until about mid-July. Around Bristol Bay, the peak of the red salmon run occurs on approximately July fourth. Once the salmon enter fresh water, they stop eating and live only off the fat reserves they have accumulated while feeding in the ocean. Depending on the species, they may travel over 2,300 miles (3,700 km). In their journey upstream, they encounter beaver dams, waterfalls and rapids, through which they must jump over or swim.

Fig. 15: Salmon fishing on the Kuskokwim River

Getting Ready

For both subsistence and commercial fishermen, getting ready for the upcoming salmon run is a necessity and often an exciting and hectic time. Commercial fishermen from as far away as Japan, Russia, San Francisco, and Seattle begin preparing for their fishing season in or near Bristol Bay. Boats must be repaired, nets checked, crews hired, supplies purchased and stored, and estimates made for the amount of fish that might be caught and the price at which they can be sold. Some commercial fishermen live in Alaskan villages or cities, and many of them store their boats around Bristol Bay. They might make a trip to the area a month or so beforehand to repair their boats and see that everything is in place. During the season, the work is hard and intense. Some season openings last for only a few hours, due to the number of fish or the duration of the run. Other season openings might last a few days or longer.

Subsistence fishermen generally fish between the intense commercial fishing openings. For subsistence fishers, "always getting ready" is a way of life. If a family goes to fish camp, it will generally travel there by boat. This means that it must purchase fuel for the round-trip, gather and purchase food supplies, and pack household supplies and fishing gear and even tents if it has no cabins. Some families might take a few days to prepare, others might take only a few hours. If the family does not go to fish camp, it probably has a drying rack and smokehouse in back of its house.

Fig. 16: Boat harbor at Bristol Bay

Fish Camp

Many coastal people of Alaska take advantage of the sizable annual salmon run to harvest a catch in preparation for winter. The critical problem facing these Alaskans is to put away enough salmon during the summer fishing season to last them to next summer's salmon season. To solve this annual problem, these skilled Alaskan fishers need to know how to catch, clean, cut, dry, smoke, pack, distribute, and store the salmon in an efficient manner.

Each cultural region of Alaska has its preferred way of organizing fish camps, catching salmon, and drying and smoking them. Even within the same cultural region, fish camps vary because of differences in salmon runs, personal preferences for organizing, catching, and processing salmon, and environmental factors. The types of houses and their arrangement, the construction of drying racks and smokehouses, the gear used to catch the salmon, the size of the camp, the amount and variety of salmon caught, and the methods of processing and preserving the catch all may differ. (Figures 17 and 18 show two different camps.)

Fig. 17: Fish camp at Lewis Point

Fish Camp Ecology

While the seasons determine the location of the camp, and in some cases also its organization and size, environmental factors, such as the type of wood available, the river's currents, and its channels also affect the overall characteristics of a camp. Often, camps that seem fairly close geographically may catch greatly differing amounts and types of salmon, depending on the currents in the river and the routes the different species take.

Fig. 18: A typical fish camp scene

Some camps are located on the coastal tundra where there are no trees, only grasses and clumps of tussocks. People bring their own wood for building and smoking, or they might gather driftwood. Other camps are located in areas where there is primarily cottonwood. Fish smoked with cottonwood will have its own distinctive flavor. The length of the drying and smoking time will also vary, depending on the weather and the size and fat content of the fish. If it is a rainy summer, the fish will take longer to dry. Bigger and fatter fish will also require a longer drying and smoking time.

The number of fish caught will depend on the size of the family and how many salmon it will need to make it through the winter. The types of salmon caught will depend on the size and type of the runs that pass by the camp. By fishing at a certain time, and by using nets with varying sized mesh, fishermen can reasonably control what type of salmon they will catch. Nets for coho salmon generally have a mesh some 6 inches (15.2 cm) wide, for reds it is usually 5 inches (12.7 cm), for chum 6.5 inches (16.5 cm), and for kings up to 8 inches (20.3 cm) wide. Near the ocean, the salmon are caught with set nets from shore, or with gill nets from small boats. In rivers, they are caught with gill nets.

Fig. 19: Fish nets

Although the salmon return at a fairly predictable time each summer, the total number of salmon that return and the distribution of the various species are far less predictable, and the number of species may vary dramatically from year to year.

Despite the many variables that determine the structure and organization of a fish camp and the amount and type of salmon caught, one characteristic holds true for all fish camps; nothing is wasted. Great care is taken to properly clean, dry, smoke and store the catch. The summer catch is a revered food all winter long.

"I never get tired of fish," says Francisca Yanez from Togiak. When she goes to college in Fairbanks, she brings enough dried salmon with her to last until her next visit home. There, she can also enjoy fish soup, fried fish, and boiled fish. "To get ready for the opening of the salmon season we need to make sure that we have our fish rack constructed and all of our gear checked and repaired, if necessary, and assembled."

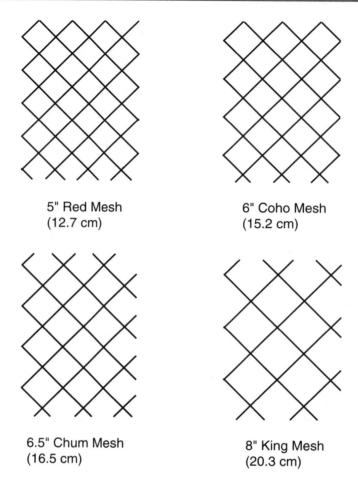

5" Red Mesh
(12.7 cm)

6" Coho Mesh
(15.2 cm)

6.5" Chum Mesh
(16.5 cm)

8" King Mesh
(20.3 cm)

Fig. 20: The above measurements are not actual size, but are proportional to one another. Also, the sizes are averages, as sizes vary region to region. Red: $4^3/4$" to $5^1/8$" (12.1 –13.0 cm); Coho: $5^3/4$" to $6^1/8$" (14.6 to 15.6 cm); King: $7^1/2$" to $8^1/2$" (19.1 to 21.6 cm)

Values and This Module

There are many important Yup'ik values associated with fishing. The elders say that during the fishing season, it is important not to catch too much as that may result in waste. At the same time, catching too little may result in hunger. If a family overharvests, it should pass the extra fish on to others in need, such as widows and the elderly. One needs to think of relatives with the most children and give them some as well. Some families put up salmon for other families who are not able to put up their own. The salmon must be given away while they are still fresh and good to eat. The important values here are to share with others, to waste nothing, and to plan ahead.

Cultural Note: Fishing for Reds in the Fall

Lorrine Nanalook, from Togiak, attends college in Fairbanks. When she was a young girl of about eleven, she used to go with her family to fish for reds in their lake. Her parents, who still live in Togiak, and her brother and his family still go fishing.

The boat ride to the lake takes about three hours. "The lake is really long and there are tall and jagged mountains on each side," explains Lorrine. "On a calm day, the water is like a mirror, but it can get choppy too." At this time, only she and her family go to this lake. "We used to just pitch a tent at the end of the lake, but now we have a cabin closer to the mouths of the creeks." The family usually spends two weeks here, fishing for reds primarily, although they also fish for trout for daily meals, and go duck hunting.

The red salmon are the biggest harvest, and they are shared amongst the family. As they are caught, Lorrine's mother splits them and hangs them to dry. Sometimes they are also taken home for additional drying. These reds are not smoked. After they have finished drying, they are stored in one gallon plastic bags in the freezer. They are eaten throughout the year, either dry or dipped in seal oil.

Fig. 21: Fish drying on the fish rack

Master Materials List

Teacher Provides

Beans—dried, of various shapes and sizes
Books—one heavy and one light weight
Cardboard—about one-foot-by-one-foot
  (30x30 cm) pieces
Coins—various sizes
Compasses
Glue
Gumdrops
Lightweight book
Paper—blank; 8.5x11 (22x28 cm) and 11x16
  (28x41 cm)
Paperclips
Poster paper
Protractors
Push pins
Rocks or pieces of wood, if students work outside
Rope—various lengths
Rulers
Scissors
Skewers
Spaghetti—dried
Stick pins
Straws
String—many rolls
Student Journals
Tape—masking and clear
Toothpicks
Transparencies—blank
Twigs
Weights—1, 2, and 5 ounce (28, 56, and 142 g) for
  a total of 50 oz (1,418 g)
Yard sticks

Package Includes

CD-ROM, Yup'ik Glossary

Posters

Three included with the module:
  Fish Racks (*Qer'at*)
  The Five Salmon Species
  Salmon Life Cycle

Blackline Masters for Transparencies

Alaska's Southwest Region
Athabaskan Fish Rack
Blackfish Story (optional)
Circumpolar North
Closed Fish Rack
Elders Planning and Establishing a Rectangular
  Base for a Fish Rack (2)
Fish Camp
Fish Camp Scenes, Today and Yesterday
Fish Drying Rack
Five Species of Pacific Salmon
Geometric Shapes with Constant Perimeter
George's Yearly Salmon Catch
Graph of Area and Length of a Rectangle—Key
Graph of Length and Width of a Rectangle
How to Derive the Area of a Parallelogram
How to Derive the Area of a Triangle
How to Derive the Area of a Trapezoid (optional)
Map of Alaska
Map of North America
Open Fish Rack *(Qer'aq)*
Rectangular Fish Racks with Perimeter of
  28 Units
Relationship of Area and Dimensions of a Rect-
  angle—Key
Relationship of Perimeter and Dimensions of a
  Rectangle—Key
Salmon Fishing
Salmon Life Cycle
Salmon Spawning: Chum, Coho, King, Pink,
  Sockeye

Sketch of Fish Rack Near the Village of Manokotak
Smokehouse
Solution to the Tiles Arrangement
Support Structure Table
The Five Salmon Species
Three Types of Support Structures
Togiak Region Resource Map
Top-down View of a Fish Rack
Two Styles of Temporary Fish Racks
Various Fish Rack Designs

Blackline Masters for Worksheets

Blackfish Story (optional)
Basic Quadrilaterals
Cm Graph Paper
Cut-out Tiles
Extended Practice (optional)
Graph of Area and Length of a Rectangle (optional)
Items at Fish Camp
Map of Lakes and Rivers of Bristol Bay
Map of Seagull Island
Phases of Salmon's Life Cycle
Properties Chart
Practice Activity
Practice with Rectangles and Constant Perimeter
Relationship of Area and Dimensions of a
    Rectangle
Relationship of Perimeter and Dimensions of a
    Rectangle
Revised Map of Seagull Island
Rules for Fish Rack Building Contest
Rules for Building a Fish Rack
Shape Cards
Three Different Sized Triangles
Vocabulary Cards (2)

Master Vocabulary List

Angle—two line segments that have a common endpoint.

Area—the measure of a bounded region on a plane.

Bisector—a line that cuts another line or an angle into two equal parts.

Center—a point equally distant from all points on the circumference of a circle.

Circle—the set of all points in a plane the same distance from the center (or a regular polygon with an infinite number of sides).

Circumference—the distance around a circle.

Circumpolar—surrounding or near either pole of the earth.

Congruent—objects having the same shape or size.

Conjecture—an inferring, theorizing, or predicting from incomplete or uncertain evidence; guesswork.

Constant—not changing; remaining the same.

Counter example—an example that proves a statement is false.

Cube—a solid with six equal square sides.

Derive—to trace from or to a source; deduce or infer.

Diagonal—a line joining two vertices of a figure that are nonadjacent.

Diameter—a line segment that goes through the center of a circle and whose end points are on the circle.

Equal—of the same quantity, size, or number.

Estimate—to guess or calculate approximately; the value of a guess or approximation.

Fish Rack—a three-dimensional structure used for drying fish.

Graph—a diagram, as a curve, broken line, series of bars, etc.

Height of a parallelogram—the perpendicular distance between the base and the opposite side.

Height of a triangle—the perpendicular distance from one side to the opposite angle.

Horizontal axis (or *x*-axis)—parallel to the plane of the horizon; not vertical.

Inscribe—to draw within a figure so as to touch in as many places as possible.

Intersect—to meet and cross at a point.

Kite—a quadrilateral that has two pairs of sides the same length, but opposite sides are not the same lengths.

Life cycle—the series of changes in form undergone by an organism in development from its earliest stage to the recurrence of the same stage in the next generation.

Line—a figure that extends in one dimension and has no endpoints.

Line segment—a figure that extends in one dimension and has two endpoints. A line segment is part of a line.

Maximum—the greatest quantity, number, or degree possible or permissible.

Measure—a standard for determining size, dimensions or capacity.

Migrate—to move from one region to another with the changes in seasons, as many birds and some fishes do.

Minimum—the smallest number, quantity, or degree.

One-dimensional—having length only, no width and no height.

Opposite—different in every way; exactly contrary.

Ordered pair—a pair of numbers used to locate a point on a graph with the first number showing the value on the horizontal axis and the second number showing the value on the vertical axis.

Parallel lines—two lines that are in the same plane and do not intersect.

Parallelogram—a quadrilateral with opposite sides parallel.

Perimeter—the measure of the outer boundary of a figure or area.

Perpendicular lines—lines that intersect to form ninety-degree angles, or right angles.

Plane—a two-dimensional figure that extends without end.

Point—a figure that does not extend in any dimension (zero dimensional).

Polygon—a closed plane figure created by three or more line segments such that each line segment intersects exactly two other segments at each endpoint and nowhere else.

Proof—anything serving or tending to establish the truth of something.

Property—a trait or characteristic of an object.

Pyramid—any structure with a square base and four sloping, triangular sides meeting at the top.

Quadrilateral—a polygon with four line segments and four angles.

Radius—a line segment with one endpoint at the center of a circle and the other endpoint on the circle.

Rectangle—a parallelogram with four right angles.

Regular polygon—a polygon that has all sides the same length and all angles the same.

Relationship—the quality or state of being related; connected.

Rhombus—a parallelogram that has four sides of equal length.

Right angle—a ninety-degree angle.

Salmon run—the movement of salmon upstream to spawn.

Scale—ratio between the dimensions of a representation and those of an object.

Spawn—to produce offspring in large numbers.

Square—a rectangle with four equal-side lengths.

Subsistence—means of support or livelihood; often the barest means of food, clothing and shelter needed to sustain life.

Table—a compact, systematic list of related details, facts, figures, etc.

Tetrahedron—see Triangular prism.

Theorem—a proposition that is not self-evident but that can be proved from accepted premises and so is established as a law or principle.

Three-dimensional—having length, width, and height.

Trapezoid—a quadrilateral with exactly one pair of parallel sides.

Triangle—a three-sided polygon.

Triangular prism—a solid figure whose bases are congruent, parallel triangles and whose other faces are parallelograms.

Two-dimensional—having length and width.

Units—the smallest whole numbers of any quantity, amount, distance or measure.

Vertical axis (or *y*-axis)—that which is perpendicular to the horizontal axis.

References

Andree, Al, as told to Jim Rearden. 1986. I sailed for salmon in Bristol Bay. *Alaska* magazine 52, no. 7 (July): 32–35, 54–55.

Barrett, Jeffrey E., et al. 2001. Children's developing knowledge of perimeter in elementary, middle, and high school. Paper presented at Annual Meeting of the American Educational Research Association, 10-14 April, in Seattle, Washington.

Brady, Philip L. 1990. Improving the reading comprehension of middle school students through reciprocal teaching and semantic mapping strategies. Ph.D. diss., University of Alaska Fairbanks.

Dick, Alan. 1997. "Cutting and drying fish." Available from the Alaska Native Knowledge Network [database online]. Fairbanks, AK [cited December 9, 1998]. Available from http://www.ankn.uaf.edu/VS/.

Lenchner, George. 1983. *Creative Problem Solving in School Mathematics*. Boston: Houghton Mifflin Co.

Lipka, Jerry, Gerald V. Mohatt, and Ciulistet Group. 1998. Transforming the Culture of Schools: Yup'ik Eskimo Examples. New Jersey: Lawrence Erlbaum Associates, Inc. Publishers.

National Council of Teachers of Mathematics (NCTM). 2000. *Principles and Standards for School Mathematics*. Reson, VA: National Council of Teachers of Mathematics.

Polya, G. 1957. *How to Solve It: A New Aspect of Mathematical Method*. 2d. ed. Princeton, NJ: Princeton University Press.

Salvadori, Mario. 1990. *The Art of Construction*. Chicago: Chicago Review Press.

Smith, D. E. 1951. *History of Mathematics*. Vol. 1, *General Survey of the History of Elementary Mathematics*. New York: Dover Publications, Inc.

Sternberg, Robert J., Elena L. Grigorenko, and Linda Jarvin. 2001. Improving reading instruction: the triarchic model. *Educational Leadership* 58, no. 6 (March): 48–52.

Vacca, Richard T., and JoAnne L. Vacca. 1999. *Content Area Reading: Literacy and Learning Across the Curriculum,* 6th ed. Boston: Longman.

Photography Credits

Anchorage Museum of History and Art:

Fish drying rack and fish camp scenes; Ward Wells Collection B83-91, WW5-1277-008 (37, 65, 198 center).

Open fish rack (qer'at); Ward Wells Collection B83-91, WW5-1277-006 (77).

Quinn, Thomas, *Various Athabaskan fish rack designs;* Fisheries Research Institute, School of Aquatic and Fishery Sciences, University of Washington (196, left; 198, bottom).

University of Alaska Fairbanks:

Nushagak salmon fishery of the early twentieth century; Romig Family Photo Collection, Accession Number 90-043-1754N, Alaska and Polar Regions Department, Rasmuson Library (11 left).

Various Athabaskan fish rack designs; Historical Photographs Collection, Accession Number 560-82, Archives, Alaska and Polar Regions Department, Rasmuson Library (71; 76; 196 right; 198 top).

Internet Resources

http://www.geocities.com/Paris/Rue/1861/etyindex.html#a

http://www.kidsdigreed.com/games.asp

http://standards.nctm.org/document/chapter6/index.htm

Section

Fishing in Southwest Alaska: A Cultural & Ecological Background

Activity 1:
Introduction to Fishing in Southwest Alaska

Along Alaska's coasts and rivers, Alaskans prepare to catch, dry, and store the bountiful run of the five species of Pacific salmon during summer. The Yup'ik along the southwest coast of Alaska have particularly large runs of salmon. To take advantage of this influx of salmon (food for the winter) entire villages may move to more advantageous locations. For example, the village of New Stuyahok, located on the Nushagak River, moves to a place called Lewis Point where the king and red salmon run in good numbers. Here people prepare their fish drying racks or build new ones and smoke their salmon to preserve them through the long winter.

The activities in this module follow the social and cultural storyline of catching and preserving salmon. Food preservation occurs in all societies. In modern western society with the preponderance of food being store-bought, most elementary-aged students may not be aware of the various ways foods are prepared and preserved. However, all students in their daily lives come into contact with preserved foods. For example, store-bought breads have preservatives in them for longer shelf life. This activity, therefore, will alert students to both their own society's and the Yup'ik people's food preservation techniques.

Goals

- To gain a basic understanding of subsistence fishing in Yup'ik culture

- To review basics of the geography of Alaska

- To estimate and compare yearly meat consumption of a student's own family to a Yup'ik family

Materials

- Poster, Fish Racks *(Qer'at)*
- Transparency, Fish Camp
- Transparency, Map of Alaska
- Transparency, Alaska's Southwest Region

- Transparency, Salmon Fishing
- Transparency, Fish Drying Rack
- Transparency, Smokehouse
- Transparency, Salmon Life Cycle
- Transparency, The Five Salmon Species
- Transparency, George's Yearly Salmon Catch

Preparation

- Prepare transparencies listed above in order
- Hang up Fish Racks *(Qer'at)* poster

Vocabulary

- Estimate—to guess or calculate approximately; the value of a guess or approximation.
- Life cycle—the series of changes in form undergone by an organism in development from its earliest stage to the recurrence of the same stage in the next generation.
- Subsistence—means of support or livelihood; often the barest means of food, clothing and shelter needed to sustain life.

Instructions

1. Ask students where their food comes from. Discuss the various responses including grocery stores or supermarkets, home gardens, farms, food banks, restaurants, hunting, fishing, gathering, etc.

2. Show the transparency Fish Camp and elicit connections between this scene and similar activities that your students may have been involved in, such as any activity that includes gathering food (berry picking), growing their own vegetables, or fishing.

3. Show the transparency Map of Alaska. Point out the major cities (Anchorage, Fairbanks, and Juneau) where life is similar to most cities in the U.S. Note the vast tracts of land not reached by highways (including the capitol). Show the transparency Alaska's Southwest Region and focus on southwest Alaska, the area in which the materials for this module were developed.

4. Point out the Fish Racks *(Qer'at)* poster and discuss how the camp is set up each summer to catch, cut, and dry salmon for the winter. Show the series of transparencies Salmon Fishing, Fish Drying Rack, and Smokehouse.

5. Explain that many people in Alaska live a subsistence lifestyle. Subsistence means they depend on food they can hunt, fish, or gather. The major salmon runs occur from May to September, and it is during these months of the year that the Yup'ik people build their fish camps to catch and process their yearly salmon supply. Ask your students to imagine that they and their families were going to purchase all the chicken or beef they needed for one year at one time. Discuss the following questions. How much would your family need? How would your family store it all? How would your family make sure their food wouldn't spoil during the year?

6. Ask the students to name some common food items that have been preserved (for example, pickles, bacon, fruit cocktail, beef jerky). Ask them to list some preserving techniques (for example, canning, salting, drying, adding certain food-preserving chemicals).

7. Show the transparencies Salmon Life Cycle and Five Salmon Species. Explain that the amount of each type of salmon passing through an area may be very different from that in other areas. Since migrating salmon return to their original birth places various species travel at different times of the year and in different waterways to get home.

8. Show the transparency Alaska's Southwest Region again and point out Akiachak. It is a small village along the Kuskokwim River. The George family who supplied the background information for this module lives here.

9. Share with the class how much salmon the George family catches in a season by showing the transparency George's Yearly Salmon Catch. Explain that these numbers are based on an estimate for a year's catch but can vary from year to year. The weight of the salmon caught also varies. This catch is for the George's immediate family as well as their extended family.

Teacher Note

The beginning four activities are meant as an introduction to fishing in southwest Alaska in order to set the stage for the module based on the Yup'ik culture. You may supplement these activities with some basic math problems such as calculating number of surviving adult salmon from the egg stage (see table on page 15) or calculating the yearly catch based on number of fish caught (see table).

George's Yearly Salmon Catch

Salmon Species	Number Caught	Approximate Weight of One Fish (lbs.)	Total Approximate Weight (lbs.)
Chum	55	7	385
King	220	15	330
Red	22	5	275
Silver	15	9	135

Fig. 1.1: Table showing an estimate of how many salmon the George family catches in a season

10. Summarize the day's discussion by reiterating the importance of salmon for the Yup'ik people and the necessity of preserving fish for an extended period of time.

11. Explain to your students that throughout the next few weeks they will be learning math through designing and building their own fish racks.

Fish Camp

Map of Alaska

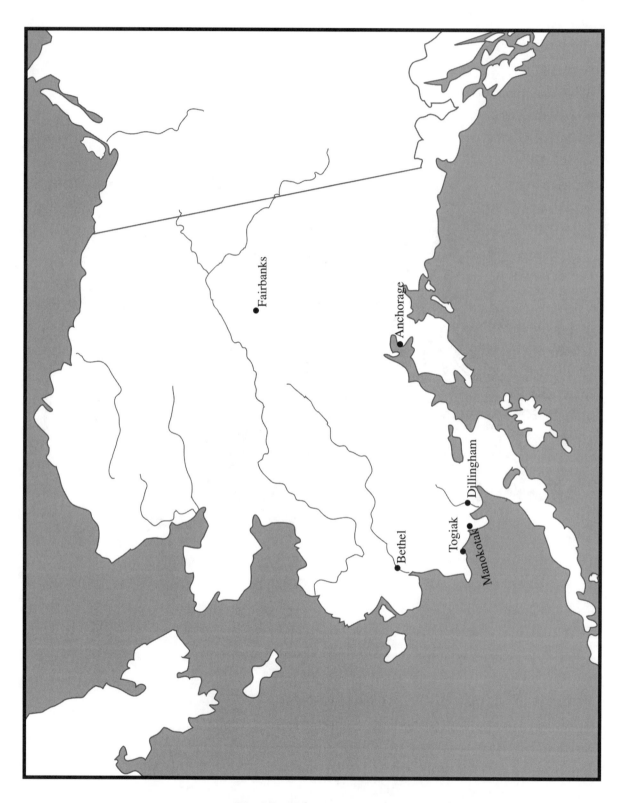

Blackline Master

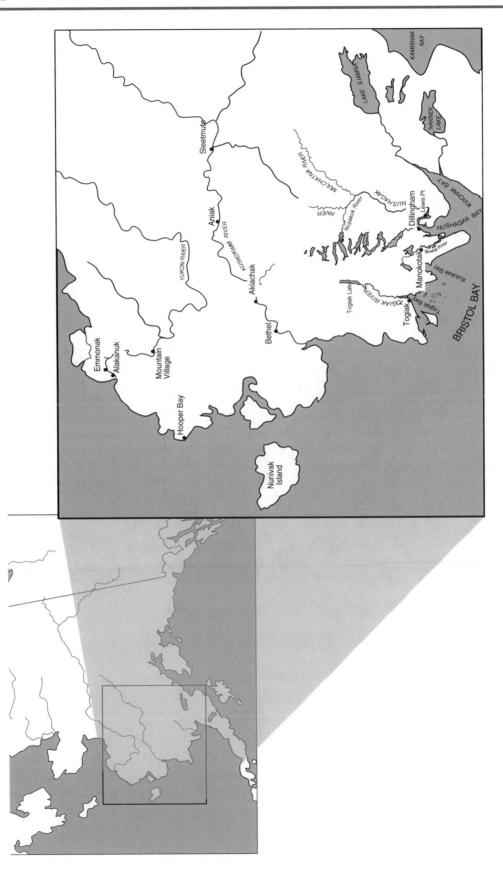

Alaska's Southwest Region

Blackline Master

Salmon Fishing

Fish Drying Rack

Smokehouse

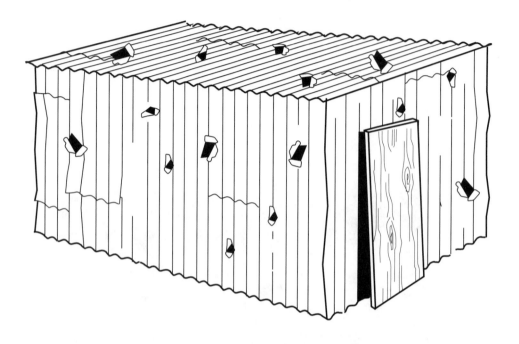

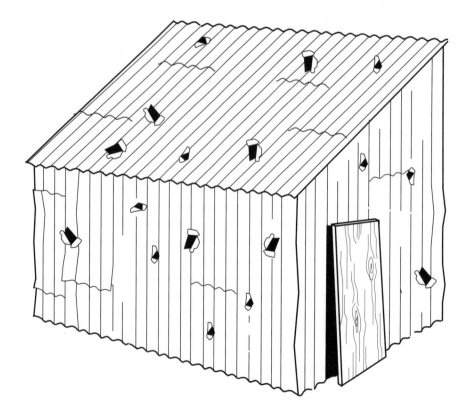

Blackline Master

Salmon Life Cycle

| EGG | ALEVIN | FRY | SMOLT | ADULT | SPAWNER |

Blackline Master

The Five Salmon Species

Chum

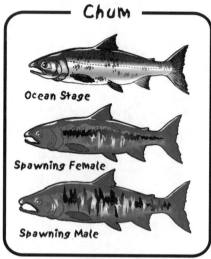

Ocean Stage

Spawning Female

Spawning Male

Coho

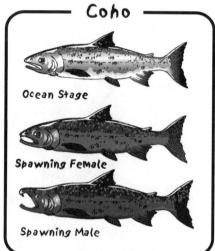

Ocean Stage

Spawning Female

Spawning Male

King

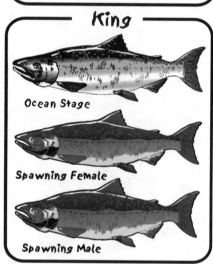

Ocean Stage

Spawning Female

Spawning Male

Pink

Ocean Stage

Spawning Female

Spawning Male

Sockeye

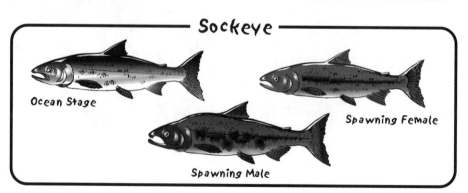

Ocean Stage

Spawning Female

Spawning Male

George's Yearly Salmon Catch

Salmon Species	Number Caught	Approximate Weight of One Fish (lbs.)	Total Approximate Weight (lbs.)
Chum	55	7	385
King	220	15	330
Red	22	5	275
Silver	15	9	135

Activity 2:
Subsistence and Location

The subsistence activities that the Yup'ik people engage in, their relative success in procuring food and materials, and the extent to which they can rely on any single subsistence resource depends largely upon their knowledge of where they live and their subsistence skills. This activity will help your students better understand the geographical location in which the Yup'ik people live, and how their location impacts their ability to procure subsistence foods and materials.

As students begin to observe relationships between land, water, and animals, they will start focusing on a key element in mathematics: relationships. Although these are not mathematical relationships, the idea of exploring relationships and observing properties forms the background and basis to all fields of mathematics and to the activities that follow in Sections 2 and 3.

Goals

- To increase your students' understanding of the geography of southwest Alaska and the geographical location and environment of the Yup'ik people

- To increase your students' understanding of maps

- To increase your students' understanding of how location impacts subsistence

Materials

- Transparency, Map of North America
- Transparency, Circumpolar North
- Transparency, Alaska's Southwest Region
- Transparency, Togiak Region Resource Map

Vocabulary

- Circumpolar—surrounding or near either pole of the earth.
- Relationship—the quality or state of being related; connected.

Instructions

1. Show your students transparency, Map of North America and ask them to find their home.

2. Ask them to find Alaska.

3. Show the transparency, Circumpolar North. Ask them to find North America, Alaska, Russia, and Greenland from this perspective. Note that the land is shown in gray.

4. Show your students the transparency of Southwest Alaska, where the fishery discussed in this module takes place. Point out Bristol Bay, the Kuskokwim Bay and River, and the Yukon River.

5. Show your students the transparency, Togiak Region Resource Map.

6. Ask your students to imagine that they are subsistence hunters and fishers. Instead of going to the grocery store to get their meat and fish, they must take it from the land. Show them on the Togiak map where fish and caribou are abundant as shown by the caribou and fish symbols. (The third symbol on the map shows beaver areas.)

7. **Challenge:** Ask your students to identify a site to build a village based on the resources shown on the map. Have them explain to class their choice of location. Record their observations on the board or on butcher paper. (Ideas around the importance of water should develop.)

Map of North America

Circumpolar North

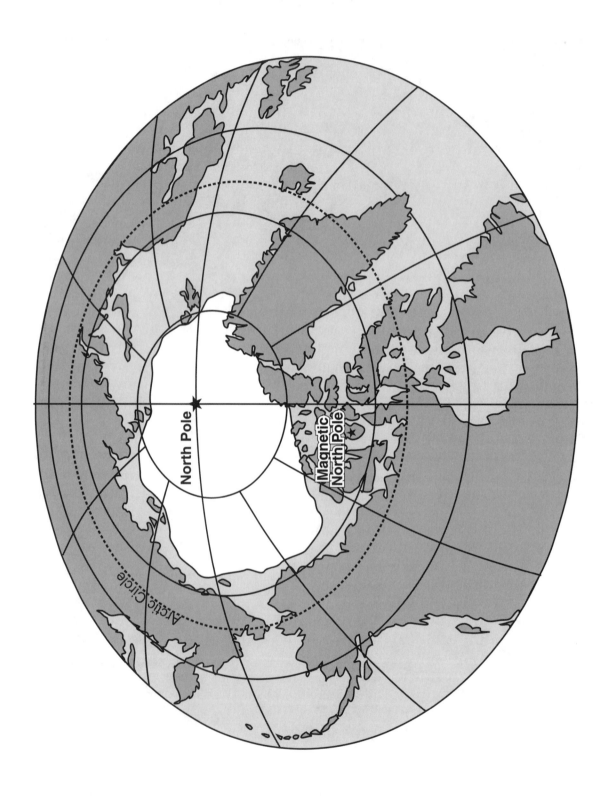

North Pole

Magnetic North Pole

Arctic Circle

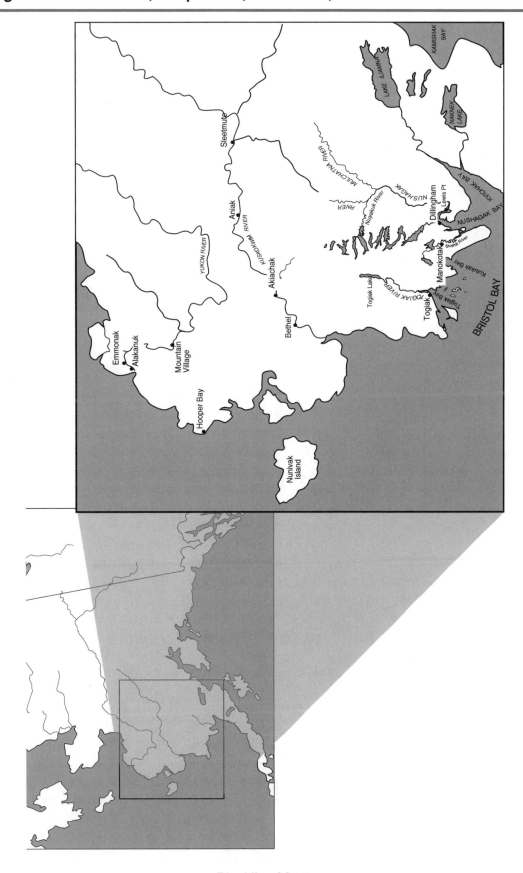

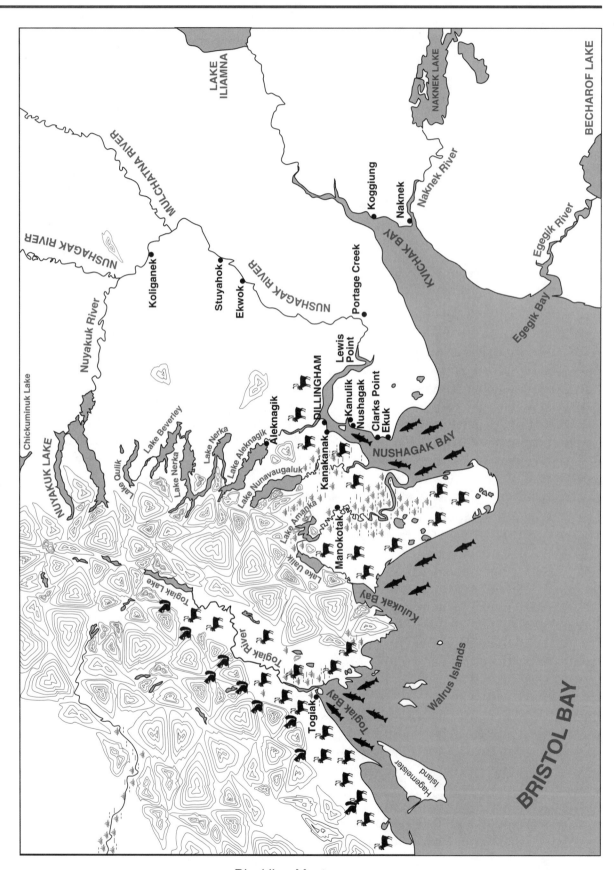

Togiak Region Resource Map

Activity 3:
The Salmon Cycle

In the preceding lessons, your students learned about subsistence fishing. Now they will explore the life cycle of the Pacific salmon because it is one of the essential subsistence foods of the Yup'ik people in southwest Alaska. Understanding the life cycle of any animal aids in harvesting and respecting that species.

Students will look for properties and relationships in the life cycle of the salmon similar to the challenge of Activity 2. In addition, they will begin a process of conjecturing that will be used throughout the remainder of the module. Here they will conjecture about biological aspects of the fish before moving into the mathematical conjectures of Sections 2 and 3.

Goals

- To gain familiarity with the different species of Pacific salmon

- To gain familiarity with the life cycle of the Pacific salmon

- To begin the process of conjecturing

Materials

- Poster, Salmon Life Cycle
- Poster, The Five Salmon Species (including the various phases of each species)
- Transparency, Five Species of Pacific Salmon
- Transparency, Salmon Life Cycle
- Five transparencies, Salmon Spawning: Chum, Sockeye, Coho, King, and Pink, as they undergo spawning changes
- Worksheet, Map of Lakes and Rivers of Bristol Bay (one per group of four students)
- Worksheet, Phases of Salmon's Life Cycle (one per group of students)
- Glue
- Scissors (one pair per student)
- Tape
- Student journals

Vocabulary

- Conjecture—an inferring, theorizing, or predicting from incomplete or uncertain evidence; guesswork.
- Migrate—to move from one region to another with the changes in seasons, as many birds and some fishes do.
- Spawn—to produce offspring in large numbers.

Instructions

1. Have students work in groups of four.

2. Pass out to each group one of each handout, Map of Lakes and Rivers of Bristol Bay and Phases of Salmon's Life Cycle.

3. Have groups conjecture where each stage of the salmon's life cycle takes place. After discussing they should cut out the drawings of the salmon in different phases and tape or glue them in the appropriate location on the map (river, lake, ocean, etc.).

4. Have each group share their maps with another group and discuss any variations in locations.

5. After groups are done discussing, share the transparency Salmon Life Cycle and further discuss the process. (For more information on the life cycle and the various species of salmon refer to the Introduction to this module.)

6. Hang up posters of Salmon Life Cycle and The Five Species of Salmon in their various life cycle phases. Show transparency of Five Species of Pacific Salmon.

7. Hand out student journals, one to each student. Explain to students that they will each keep a record of their work during this module by using journals. Have them place a heading on the first page related to Salmon Life Cycle.

8. Have your students observe differences between the five salmon species, write their observations in their journals, and share their observations with the class.

9. Show the transparency Chum with the ocean-going colors and the spawning phase on the overhead. Explain the migrating process to the students if they don't already know about it.

10. Show the series of transparencies, Sockeye, Coho, King, and Pink. Have students make observations about the spawning salmon among and between different species. Discuss their ideas.

11. Have students write conjectures in their journals as to why the salmon go through these physical changes during migration and spawning.

12. Collect journals or have students store them for the next activity.

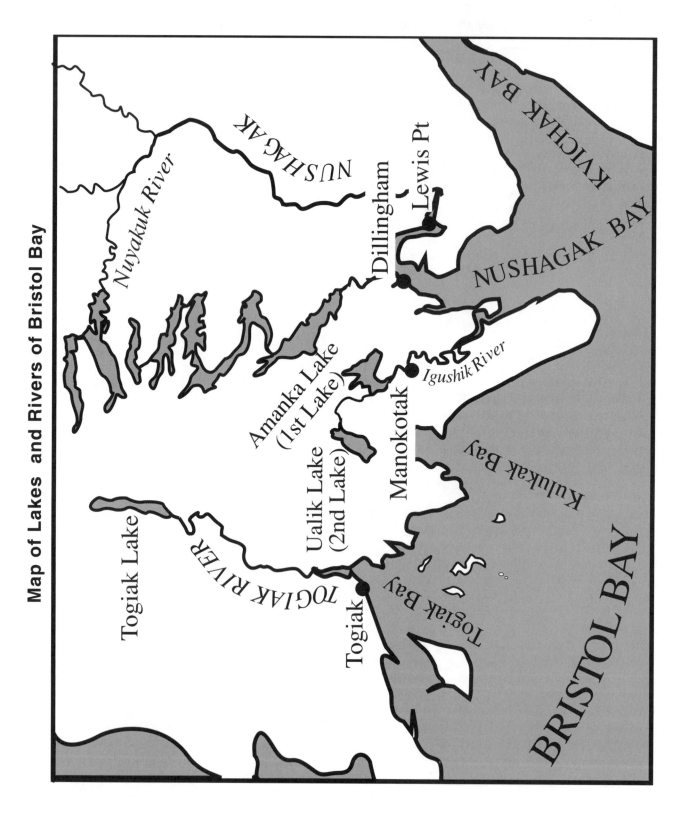

Map of Lakes and Rivers of Bristol Bay

Phases of Salmon's Life Cycle

Salmon egg

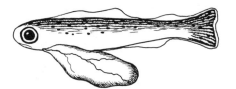

Salmon alevin

Salmon fry

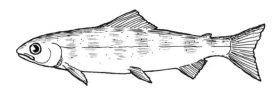

Salmon smolt

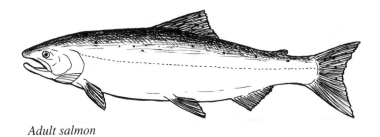

Adult salmon

Salmon Life Cycle

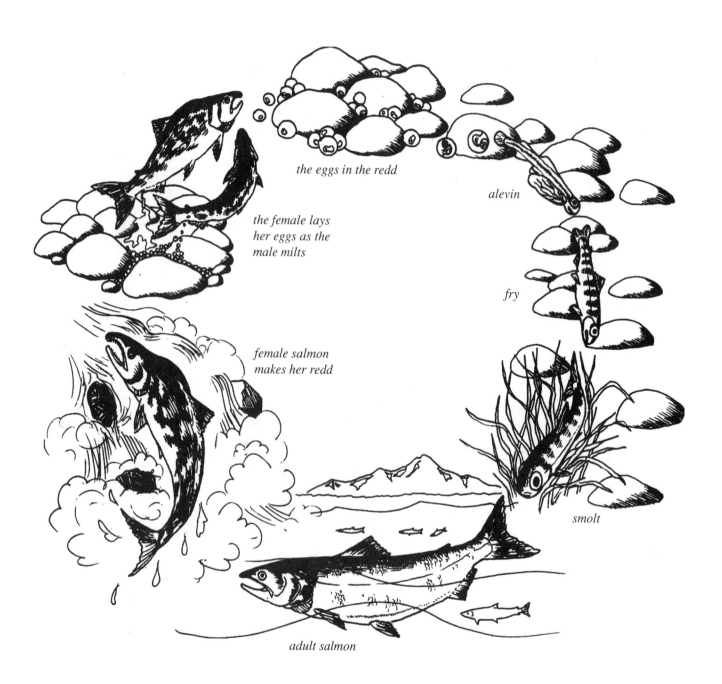

the eggs in the redd

alevin

the female lays her eggs as the male milts

fry

female salmon makes her redd

smolt

adult salmon

Five Species of Pacific Salmon

Pink (Humpback) Salmon

Coho (Silver) Salmon

Chum Salmon

Sockeye (Red) Salmon

King (Chinook) Salmon

Blackline Master

Chum

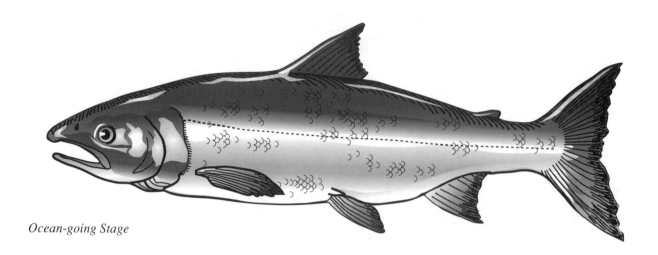

Ocean-going Stage

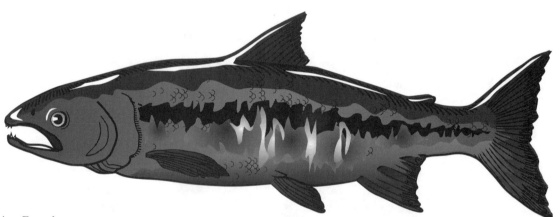

Spawning Female

Spawning Male

Blackline Master

Sockeye

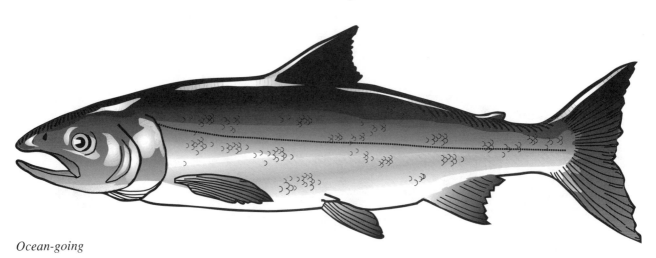

Ocean-going

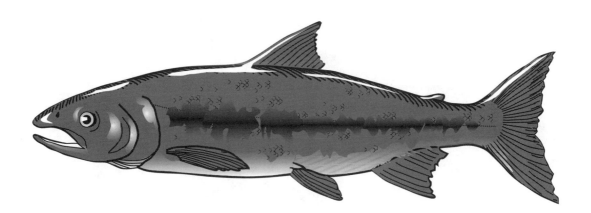

Spawning Female

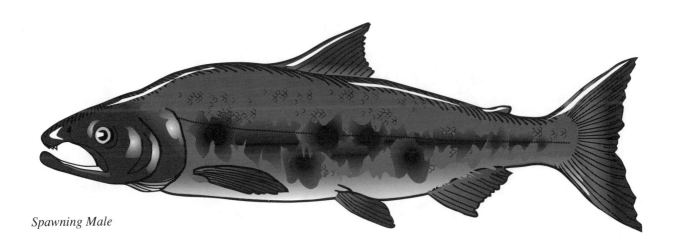

Spawning Male

Blackline Master

Coho

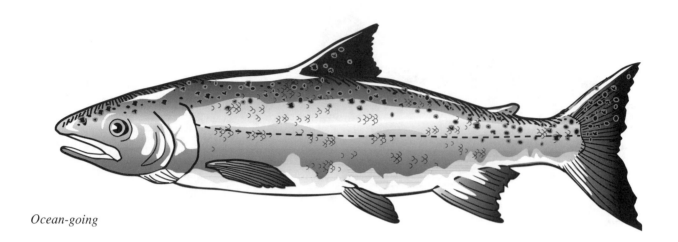

Ocean-going

Spawning Female

Spawning Male

Blackline Master

King

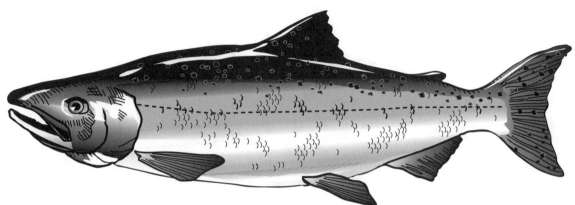

Ocean-going

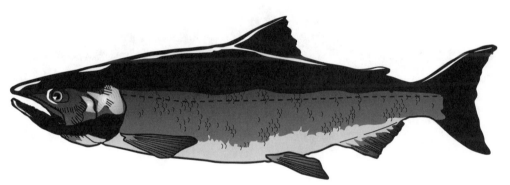

Spawning Female

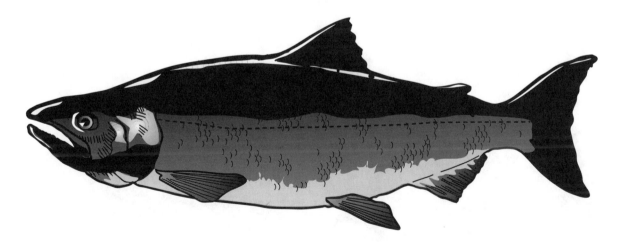

Spawning Male

Pink

Ocean-going

Spawning Female

Spawning Male

Blackline Master

Activity 4:
Getting Ready

It is summer in Alaska and the mature salmon are returning from the Pacific Ocean to the freshwater rivers, streams and lakes to spawn. The Yup'ik, as well as other indigenous peoples of Alaska, must prepare their fish camps for the summer harvest, as they have for generations. Important components of getting ready are to make sure that the camp is orderly (refer to "The Blackfish Story" at the end of this activity), and that the fish rack is stable and will be able to hold the anticipated catch of salmon.

The following activity, adapted from everyday Yup'ik life, illustrates the importance of being prepared. In this case, communities, families, and individuals up and down the coast of Alaska prepare to harvest the incoming salmon. The nature of the problem, the ways of solving it (particularly its emphasis on visualization), and the ways of instructing students are based on traditional Yup'ik ways and knowledge but have been adapted to classroom use.

Real-world mathematics, or everyday mathematics, forms an important connection between students' lives and school mathematics. Yup'ik Eskimo everyday problems, unfamiliar to most students, offer new challenges to which students can apply problem-solving skills, mathematical and practical knowledge.

Goals

- To gain understanding in the ecology of subsistence and commercial harvesting of salmon

- To gain understanding of the importance of preparation to a successful fishing season

- To gain understanding of maps

Materials

- Transparency, Fish Camp Scenes, Today and Yesterday
- Transparency or worksheet, The Blackfish Story (optional)
- Student journals

Vocabulary

• Salmon run—the movement of salmon upstream to spawn.

Instructions

1. Read the following text to your students:

    Imagine that you are living in a different time, not so long ago, when you and your family have to gather your own food. It's a time without supermarkets, motorized transportation, or electrical power.

    From your seat, look out the classroom window. Now close your eyes. Slowly remove all buildings, roads, and other human-made structures. Fill in the scene with what you imagine the environment looked like before all those things were built. What do you see?

2. Have your students report on what they imagined; write out some of their responses on the board.

3. Remind your students of subsistence fish camps. Show them the transparency Fish Camp Scenes, Today and Yesterday, which features photos of tundra, rivers, a smokehouse, and a drying rack.

4. Explain to students that in summer and fall, the salmon run provides the surest and most abundant supply of food for the approaching lean months, so being ready is of the utmost importance. According to Alan Dick (from McGrath), old timers say:

    Fish as if you wouldn't catch any animals all winter. Then, if you do catch something you will do well, but if you don't catch any animals, you will get tired of fish, but you won't starve. (Alan Dick. "Cutting and Drying Fish." Online. December 9, 1998.)

5. Read Nastasia Wahlberg's personal story of how she gets ready ("Getting Ready").

6. Hand out the student journals. Have them place a heading on the next empty page related to "Getting Ready." Now that the students know how Nastasia prepares, ask them what they would do to get ready for the fishing season. Have them write their responses in their journals. (Responses may include net mending, repair and or construction of fish rack and smokehouse, putting the boat in good order, and collecting other important items.) Note some of their responses on the board.

Getting Ready

Nastasia Wahlberg and her family have a fish camp near Bethel. Although Nastasia now lives in Fairbanks, she grew up in Bethel and still tries to go home in the summer to work in her family's fish camp. By June 1, the excitement of the season starts. The boat is packed with gear, and the family sets off across the Kuskokwim River, near their village, to clean up the camp and prepare for three months of fishing. Because this part of Alaska is located in the sub-Arctic, the sun shines day and night throughout most of the summer.

By the time we've gone across, the kids are always excited because they get to stay up late or go fishing with a pole. We all stay up late; there's so much to do. Everybody's anxious to get out of town. There's more freedom for the kids to play, but we still have to watch them closely. There's the wilderness, the river, and the tides. And we always have to watch out for the boat. We don't want it to get stranded or damaged by the tide.

My father used to make a list of everything we needed. My mother made one in her own way. She made sure that we brought enough food. And our knives, the ulus, are very important. We made sure we had our sharpening supplies. Also Blazo [a petroleum fuel used in camp stoves], a Coleman stove, rubber boots, tennis shoes and rain pants. We wear rain pants when we're cutting fish.

At camp after cutting and cleaning the fish, we'll take a coffee break. And we have a cook or two and someone to watch the kids. Usually it's one of the younger girls or Grandma.

The person who catches the first king salmon is big news. People spread the news via radio or CB, or by boat up and down the Kuskokwim River. Before fish camp [when we were fishing from home], the first salmon that we get, if the family has enough, we bring to others. Especially to elders and those who have a hard time getting their own fish.

Cultural Note

Not wasting is a core Yup'ik value. This story, in which the blackfish chooses the trap and its owner, illustrates this value, and the relationship between people and animals. The fisher does not trap the fish, but her skill and care show that she is worthy of receiving the blackfish.

7. If possible, show your students a fish net and different sized meshes, for example one for king salmon and one for pink salmon or red salmon (see Figs. 19 and 20 in the Introduction).

8. Read your students "The Blackfish Story," or have students take turns reading each paragraph.

9. Have your students discuss this story. Have them pay particular attention to the important Yup'ik values it reflects, i.e. food is to be revered, not wasted. Relate elements of the story to getting ready. Some questions you could ask are:

    *   Why didn't the blackfish like the first trap?
    *   What did it like so much about the second trap?
    *   Why did the blackfish want to be caught?
    *   What does the blackfish's attitude say about the Yup'ik's relationship to the animals they depend on for survival?

10. Collect journals or have students store them. Explain that part of getting ready each day while working on this module includes having their journals ready to use.

Looking Ahead

Students should now have a good feel for the cultural and ecological background needed to understand one aspect of Yup'ik life—subsistence fishing. In the next section, students will observe elders building a fish rack, either in person or through the photos included on transparencies. Through that process students will investigate the properties of rectangles and other related shapes. This mathematical diversion will provide students with the information needed to move from the cultural and real-world situation to the ideal and mathematical situation. This will establish them in the process of mathematical modeling of the fish racks.

Fish Camp Scenes, Today and Yesterday

Frederick George at the door of his smokehouse

Tundra

Fish hanging to dry, Bethel 1951

Sunset on the Kuskokwim River

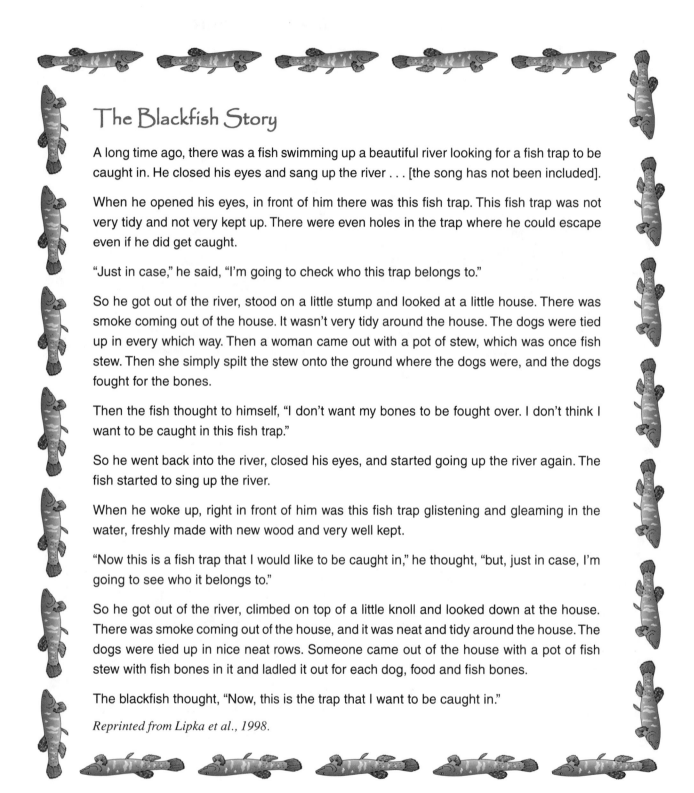

The Blackfish Story

A long time ago, there was a fish swimming up a beautiful river looking for a fish trap to be caught in. He closed his eyes and sang up the river . . . [the song has not been included].

When he opened his eyes, in front of him there was this fish trap. This fish trap was not very tidy and not very kept up. There were even holes in the trap where he could escape even if he did get caught.

"Just in case," he said, "I'm going to check who this trap belongs to."

So he got out of the river, stood on a little stump and looked at a little house. There was smoke coming out of the house. It wasn't very tidy around the house. The dogs were tied up in every which way. Then a woman came out with a pot of stew, which was once fish stew. Then she simply spilt the stew onto the ground where the dogs were, and the dogs fought for the bones.

Then the fish thought to himself, "I don't want my bones to be fought over. I don't think I want to be caught in this fish trap."

So he went back into the river, closed his eyes, and started going up the river again. The fish started to sing up the river.

When he woke up, right in front of him was this fish trap glistening and gleaming in the water, freshly made with new wood and very well kept.

"Now this is a fish trap that I would like to be caught in," he thought, "but, just in case, I'm going to see who it belongs to."

So he got out of the river, climbed on top of a little knoll and looked down at the house. There was smoke coming out of the house, and it was neat and tidy around the house. The dogs were tied up in nice neat rows. Someone came out of the house with a pot of fish stew with fish bones in it and ladled it out for each dog, food and fish bones.

The blackfish thought, "Now, this is the trap that I want to be caught in."

Reprinted from Lipka et al., 1998.

Section

Establishing a Fish Rack:

The Geometry of a Rectangle

Activity 5:
Elder Demonstration

Now that the fishing season is upon us it is time to get ready. As we return to our fish camp, we notice that we need to rebuild our fish rack. The previous year's harsh winter caused frost heaves, and the fish rack structure is no longer stable. We must build a new one. The first problem to solve as we get ready is to make sure that the new fish rack structure will be stable.

Typically, Yup'ik elders teach through demonstration, and they expect interested persons to learn through observation. If an elder is not available to teach these skills, the classroom teacher will need to demonstrate them by using the included illustrations/transparencies that show a few different fish racks, different views of fish racks, and the steps taken by one elder to find the corners and the center of the structure. There are many different designs depending upon local conditions, personal knowledge, and preferences.

Before a new fish rack can be built, a suitable piece of level ground must be found. Prior to constructing the fish rack some elders establish four corners where the posts will be placed thus defining the width and length of the structure. The method outlined below was chosen because of its particular connections to mathematics. These include how to establish the center so that the structure will be stable, how to measure the length and width, and how to visualize the finished fish rack.

Fig. 5.1: Sketch of a fish rack near Manokotak

Goals

- To introduce a variety of fish rack designs

- To observe how elders establish the rectangular base of a fish rack

Materials

- Poster, Fish Racks *(Qer' at)*
- Transparency, Sketch of Fish Rack Near the Village of Manokotak
- Transparency, Athabaskan Fish Rack
- Transparency, Open Fish Rack *(Qer'aq)*
- Transparency, Closed Fish Rack *(Talicivik)* [shaded fish rack with roof]
- Transparency, Top-down View of a Fish Rack
- Transparencies, Elders Planning and Establishing a Rectangular Base for a Fish Rack
- Student journals

Vocabulary

- Fish rack—a three-dimensional structure used for drying fish.
- Measure—a standard for determining size, dimensions or capacity.

Instructions

If an elder is available to your class, ask him or her, or another knowledge-able person, to share stories about building fish racks and other knowledge learned through life experience. Students should listen, observe, and care-fully follow the elder's instructions.

1. Have the elder show the students how to find a suitable piece of land on which to erect a fish rack.

2. If the elder orients the fish rack toward the prevailing wind, encour-age him to explain why, that orienting the rack toward the wind al-lows the fish to dry faster.

3. There are many ways to establish the corners of the fish rack. Observe how the elder finds the corners and center of the fish rack base.

Fig. 5.2: Athabaskan fish rack

If an elder is not available then follow the instructions noted below.

4. Remind the students of the importance of getting ready including the importance of having one's fish racks ready. Ask them to list a few steps that might be taken to prepare for the upcoming fishing season.

5. Show the students the following transparencies of fish racks. Ask them to pay attention to the different styles and to the geometric shapes that are part of a fish rack. Also point out the hanging poster, Fish Racks *(Qer' at)* and the various fish racks shown there.
   • Sketch of a Fish Rack Near the Village of Manokotak
   • Athabaskan Fish Rack
   • Open Fish Rack *(Qer' aq)*
   • Closed Fish Rack *(Talicivik)*

6. Ask the students, "What geometric shape do these various fish racks form on the ground?" Have them respond.

Teacher Note

Stress that the method of building a rack used by the elders is one possible method out of many. Remember that building a fish rack is *not engineering or formal mathematics;* it is practical building and everyday mathematics. This means that visual estimating and getting your structure sufficiently accurate is good enough in real world application. "Good enough" and "sufficient" means that it will stand, it will hold the weight of the salmon, it will be stable, and it will last a long enough time. It is possible that built in this way, the fish rack may not exactly be made with ninety-degree angles or perfectly equal opposite sides. However, this is the difference between everyday knowledge, including Yup'ik cultural knowledge, and pure mathematics. This module shows in various ways the relationship between these two different domains.

7. Share the following information, provided by Yup'ik elders, with your class:

    •   Henry Alakayak from Manokotak, Alaska stresses how important it is to be able to visualize the fish rack before beginning construction. In this way, he is able to determine which types of trees he will need for the posts, beams and poles of the fish rack. First he thinks about how long the poles needed to hang the fish should be so he knows where the corners or posts of his fish rack will be. He then selects the trees and branches that seem suitable and are available. He approximates the tree lengths, then adjusts them to the fish rack by cutting them into equal lengths. Finally, he visualizes how wide the fish rack should be when completed.

    •   The elders agree that "the ancestors used to think about how many fish they were going to catch for the size of the fish rack." This means that the ancestors visualized how big a finished fish rack needed to be based on how many fish they predicted would be needed for their families. They made their predictions without counting individual fish, but by visualizing the shape and volume of the fish.

    •   Mike Toyukak, a Yup'ik fisherman from southwest Alaska, remembers a fish rack experience: "At first we had the ends of our drying racks facing east/west. During that time there was not much air circulating. After the fish rack fell down, we rebuilt it facing north/south and the fish dried better even if it was raining." Mike learned through experience that the orientation of the fish rack toward the wind is *one* important factor in drying salmon.

8. Show the transparency Top-down View of a Fish Rack (Fig. 5.3). If the students have any difficulty in perceiving the rectangular base, ask them to name other, more familiar objects/structures that also have a rectangular base. For instance, many buildings have a rectangular shape.

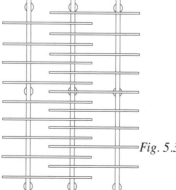

Fig. 5.3: Top-down view of a fish rack

9. Tell the students that the next set of transparencies show a group of elders planning and then establishing a rectangular base for the fish rack that they will build. Pay attention to their method of establishing a rectangle.

(a) This group of elders first discusses possible construction techniques (Fig. 5.4). A firm and level piece of ground must be chosen and then the center should be marked.

(b) Nonstandard forms of measurement are used to determine the size of the structure. Body measures like the measure of a stride or the space between outstretched arms are used to estimate the size and spacing of the fish rack. In this case, a rope is used as a tool to estimate the length of the structure (Fig. 5.5). The elders tie a knot in the rope to mark significant lengths.

(c) The rope is also used to estimate the width of the structure (Fig. 5.6).

(d) The elders measure the diagonal (Fig. 5.7).

Fig. 5.4: Henry Alakayak, Sam Ivan, and Joshua Phillip planning a fish rack

Fig. 5.5: Elders use a rope to determine the length. Arrows indicate the corners of the future fish rack

Fig. 5.6: Elders use a rope to determine the width. Arrows indicate the corners of the future fish rack

Fig. 5.7: Elders measuring the diagonal distance

(e) There is a need to recheck the distances in order to make sure that a rectangle is established. The location of the corners is adjusted accordingly (Fig. 5.8).

(f) Digging 3-foot (.9 m) deep post holes for the foundation will help ensure that the structure will stand in the harsh Alaskan environment (Fig. 5.9).

(g) The four posts sticking out of the ground are the corners of the future fish rack (Fig. 5.10).

10. Ask the students to write in their journals about the process they observed and why the elders took so much care in creating the rectangular base.

Fig. 5.8: Rechecking the diagonal distance.
Arrows indicate the corners

Fig. 5.9: Digging the holes for the
posts

Fig. 5.10: Putting in the posts and beams for
the fish rack

Sketch of a Fish Rack Near the Village of Manokotak

Athabaskan Fish Rack

Open Fish Rack *(Qer'aq)*

Closed Fish Rack *(Talicivik)*

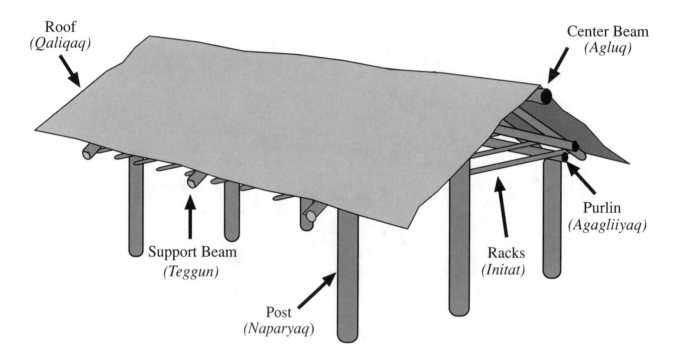

Roof
(Qaliqaq)

Center Beam
(Agluq)

Support Beam
(Teggun)

Purlin
(Agagliiyaq)

Post
(Naparyaq)

Racks
(Initat)

Top-down View of a Fish Rack

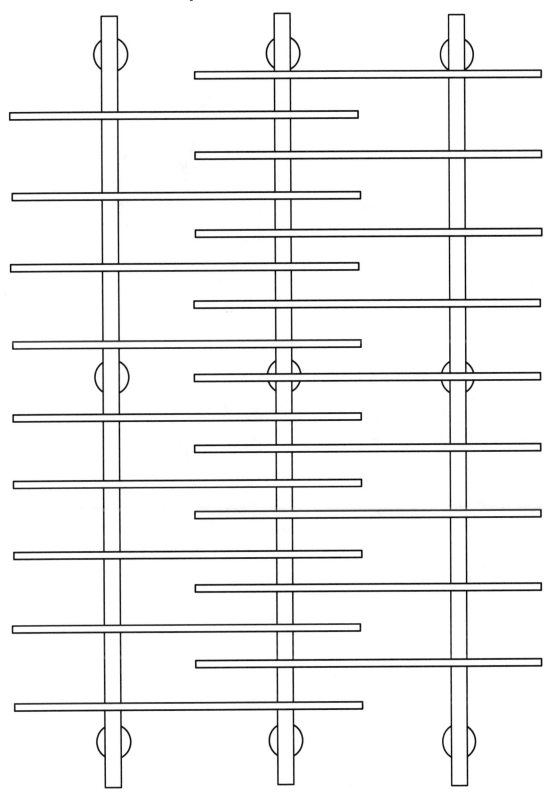

Blackline Master

Elders Planning and Establishing a Rectangular Base
for a Fish Rack

Henry Alakayak, Sam Ivan and Joshua Phillip planning a fish rack.

Elders use a rope to determine the length. Arrows indicate the corners of the future fish rack.

Elders use a rope to determine the width. Arrows indicate the corners of the future fish rack.

Elders measuring the diagonal distance.

Elders Planning and Establishing a Rectangular Base
for a Fish Rack (p. 2)

Rechecking the diagonal distance. Arrows indicate the corners.

Digging the holes for the posts.

Putting in the posts and beams for the fish rack.

Activity 6:
Students Establish a
Rectangular Base

In this activity students will construct the rectangular base of a structure by establishing the four corners of a rectangle on the ground. The teacher will need to provide enough space, 9 feet x 12 feet (2.7 to 3.7 m) per group, either in the hallway or preferably outside, for the students to explore different strategies. Finding the corners and the center of this rectangular base differs considerably from drawing a rectangle on paper and finding its corners and center. On paper, precision is easily accomplished. On the ground, it is not so easy to be precise, so students learn to settle for "almost accurate" or good enough. These differences relate directly to the differences between everyday mathematics and formal mathematics. The action of solving this problem by doing rather than with paper and pencil deepens the connection between mathematics and Yup'ik ways of knowing.

In the previous activity, students were shown several fish rack designs. The most common shape is rectangular. In this activity, students will explore methods of ascertaining that the shape they make on the ground comes close to resembling a rectangle.

Keep in mind that everyday language forms people's notion of shape, which may not fit the mathematical definition. Everyday language expresses a partial description of the properties or paints a picture of a shape. For example, in the Yup'ik language, the word for square is *kangirenqellria,* which literally means "corner." This gives us a picture of ninety-degree corners. The modern Yup'ik word for square is borrowed from Russian, *yaasiigenqellria,* which means "box." However, this word conjures up a picture of a cube and not a two-dimensional corner. The word for rectangle is *taksurenqellria* and means "one that is long." This gives the picture of a stereotypical rectangle. In mathematics, we define a rectangle as a closed four-sided figure with opposite sides parallel. Thus in Western mathematics, the square is a special case of the rectangle, whereas in the Yup'ik language the rectangle is special. By challenging students' everyday knowledge of these basic math terms, they may at first resist until they begin to appreciate the importance of properties defining shape.

Teacher Note

By learning through demonstration and practice without using Western instrumentation, your students are taking a tour through the history of mathematics. As they explore the relationship between width, length, and diagonal they will be confronted with problems that people all over the world faced as they were developing their geometry. (See the Historical Note that follows for additional information on the cross-cultural and historical roots of geometry and pure mathematics.)

Goals

• To establish a rectangular base on the ground

• To use nonstandard forms of measurement

• To introduce the concept of proofs through physical demonstration

• To define a rectangle

Materials

• A rope 7.5 feet (2.3 m) in length for each group of three students
• Yard sticks
• Protractors
• Masking tape or stick pins
• String (one per group)
• Rocks or pieces of wood for marking the center and corners, if students work outside
• Poster paper
• Student journals

Duration

• Two to three class periods.

Vocabulary

These terms may come up while students construct a rectangle. Encourage class discussion of these terms and ask students to write their own definitions in their journals.

• Bisector—a line that cuts another line or an angle into two equal parts.
• Congruent—objects having the same shape and size.
• Diagonal—a line joining two vertices of a figure that are nonadjacent.
• Intersect—to meet and cross at a point.
• Line—a figure that extends in one dimension and has no endpoints.
• Parallel lines—two lines that are in the same plane and do not intersect.
• Parallelogram—a quadrilateral with opposite sides parallel.
• Plane—a two-dimensional figure that extends without end.
• Point—a figure that does not extend in any dimension (zero-dimensional).
• Proof—anything serving or tending to establish the truth of something.

- Rectangle—a parallelogram with four right angles.
- Right angle—a ninety-degree angle.
- Square—a rectangle with four equal side lengths.
- Theorem—a proposition that is not self-evident but that can be proved from accepted premises and so is established as a law or principle.

Instructions

1. Ask students to get into groups of three. Hand out student journals if students do not already have them.

2. Ask students to draw a rectangle in their journal.

3. When the students have completed that task, ask them to write their definition for a rectangle. Have the students make believe that they are writing their definition for a third grader. This means that they should make few assumptions and write clear sentences explaining what they think.

4. As a practical application of working with rectangles, ask if students in your class have had experience building doll houses, bird houses, shacks, etc. If so, have them briefly describe their experience to the class.

5. Tell each group that they can choose to use any of the materials you've set out for them from the list of materials. Hand out colored pins or tape so that the students may mark the different points on the ground that they establish. If they are working outside, they may use rocks or pieces of wood to mark the corners and the center.

6. **Challenge.** Ask the students to find the four corners of a rectangle. Let the students know that they can use any of the material that they need to find the four corners for a structure that will be approximately 9 feet by 12 feet (2.7 by 3.7 m). Give the students fifteen to twenty minutes to establish the rectangular base, keeping in mind the dimensions are less important than the process.

7. If, after a reasonable period of time, students are having difficulty finding the corners, have one group that is proceeding well demonstrate for the others, or provide a few hints and/or brief demonstration on how to find one corner.

Teacher Note

Observe the different groups and how they try to construct their rectangles. If students chose to use the 7.5 foot (2.3 m) rope, then they may have trouble establishing the four corners as some students try to solve the problem "literally," that is they want the rope to be equal to the sides of the rectangle. Since the rope appears to be "too short" some students get stuck at this point. For example, some students said, "The rope is only about 8 feet (2.4 m) long. But it has to be 12 feet (3.7 m) long. I thought we had to use the rope to make the rectangle."

Another group ran into problems because the rope was not long enough to measure from one point to another but they came up with a solution. They decided to use one student's foot. They discussed the question, "How long is your foot?" They talked about differences in different individuals' foot size. They decided to take nine steps to mark the width. When asked why, they said: "It is probably 9 feet (2.7 m) across."

Limitations exist for each method of constructing a rectangle. When using equal diagonals, the shape could become an isosceles trapezoid if the property that opposite sides must be the same length is ignored. On the other hand, if opposite sides are established to be the same length then a parallelogram may be created if care is not used to create right angles. Lastly, connecting points on a circle without forming parallel sides will not produce a rectangle.

Other students may continually change their point of reference as they try to establish the center and/ or the corners. By changing their point of reference, they cannot form a rectangular base. For example, a student group proceeded to measure from the center out to the midpoint of one of the sides and then from a corner to the midpoint of a different side. Their point of reference changed and they had to sort out in which direction their rectangle would lie.

This exercise provides you with a good opportunity to observe the students' communication and then to provide hints or to briefly demonstrate correct ways of completing the exercise. All students are expected to take part in visually estimating and physically approximating the layout of the rectangle.

8.   Have groups pair up. Each group should explain its method of verification of a rectangle to the other. This gives the students practice in putting their actions into words.

9.   **Discuss.** Ask each group to state or show any of the properties of a rectangle they discovered or to explain how they knew they had a rectangle. Have students create a poster using poster paper with all their properties and proofs of rectangles so far.

This may be a good stopping point for the day. If you choose to stop here, then use step 10 as a good review for the beginning of the next class.

10. Have your students work in their groups of three for ten minutes to answer the following. Imagine you were invited on TV to show people how to make a fish rack. What would you say and do to make sure that people remember the most important points of making a fish rack? Have each group share their ideas with the class.

11. Compare students' work on the poster with the first three theorems of a rectangle listed in the Mathematics Note at the end of this activity. (The last two theorems are more difficult to discover.) Mark the theorems that students did NOT share from their discoveries in your own notebook (this is not for public display). Do NOT tell students or show students the Mathematics Note. Instead, have students get back into their groups. Provide each group with a hint to lead them into discovering one of the theorems missed so far.

    Hints
    For the Diagonal Theorem ask:
     Have you looked at the diagonals?
    For the Perpendicular Bisector Theorem ask:
     Have you considered the midpoints?
    For the Inscribed Rectangle Theorem ask:
     How could this relate to a circle?
     or
     What's the relationship between the diagonals and a circle?

12. After groups have had ample time to discover, have them each present their methods and results to the class. Have them add any new properties or proofs of rectangles to their posters and name them.

Fig. 6.1: Students checking their rectangle by measuring the diagonals with string

13. **Debrief.** Ask the students to reread in their journals their earlier definition of a rectangle. Ask them to modify their definition based on what they have learned.

14. Move about the room, observing the students' work. Take this opportunity to help students develop their own definitions by reflecting on the properties discovered.

15. Have the students share their modified definitions with the class.

Fig. 6.2: Students marking the midpoint of one side of a rectangle

Exploration

If you have circular geoboards hand one out to each group of students. Hand out one seven-inch piece of string to each group. Have the students review the physical proof of inscribing a rectangle in a circle. Note that the circular geoboard has a pin located in each corner near the edge of the board. The four pins represent the four corners of the board or a square. The students should be able to use the string as a radius, tying it to the center and stretching it till it touches one of the pins. Then, they should be able to form an arch with the string circumscribing a circle around the square. The string radius should touch each of the four points/pins.

Leslie Dolan, a sixth-grade teacher in Fairbanks, Alaska, stated that "when they discovered the proofs for rectangles using their geoboards, my students seemed to appreciate being able to see these proofs before applying them." The students said, "Wow, look at this. It really works. A circle encloses a rectangle." Leslie also mentioned that "this was also a great way to go over vocabulary such as radius, diameter, diagonal, and circumference."

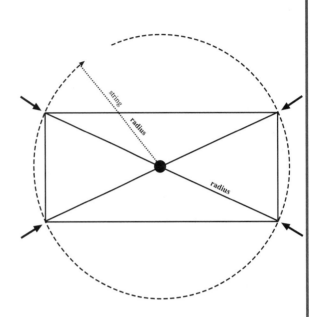

Fig. 6.3: A rectangle inscribed in a circle

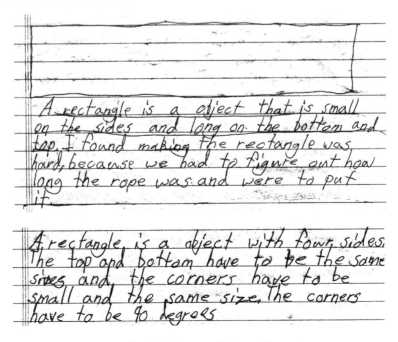

Fig. 6.4: An example of student work from a journal

Math Note

The Origins of Math Terms

It may be beneficial for you as the teacher to see a brief introduction into the origin of the math terms used here. Often seeing where the words evolved from aids in understanding students misconceptions of shapes or difficulties in distinguishing properties

Square is derived from the Latin phrase *Exquadrare,* like a quadratic. Over time the term was contracted into its present form, and came to mean the regular quadrilateral. The word is also the root of the military term squadron, which originally meant a fighting square from the early practice of fighting in square formations.

Rectangle is derived from the Latin word *rectus,* which is derived from the Greek term *ortho* which was used to mean both straight and erect. We see the imprint of rectus in many math words and common language with both the straight and erect meanings. As languages blended in the middle ages, *rectus* became "recht" and eventually became our word for "right" and for the right angle. The idea of vertical as the "right" position led to the use of right as proper or good. We see this in words like correct, which means, literally, to make straight (or right).

Angle comes from the Latin root *angulus,* a sharp bend. As with many g sounds the transfer from Latin to the German and English languages switched to a *k* spelling. The word ankle is from the same root. Two rays with a common endpoint form an angle.

Rhombus was used by Euclid in the form of the word *rombos.* In his translation Heath says it is apparently drawn from the Greek word *rembw,* to turn round and round.

Polygon is from the Greek roots *poli* (many) and *gonus* (knees) and translates as "many angled." The relation between knee and angle relates to the flexed position of the knee.

Line has its roots hidden in the genus of the flax plant, lenum, and the fibers of the plant that were spun together to make a thread called linen. The idea of stretching the thread to mark a straight segment between two points leads easily to the name of the imaginary one-dimensional figure with no endpoints.

Trapezoid originally comes from the Greek word for table. Today, in the USA, the term trapezoid refers to a quadrilateral with one pair of sides parallel as well as with NO parallel sides.

Area is a general term for a measure of two-dimensional space and comes unchanged from the Latin. The more common meaning of area applies, as it did 2,000 years ago, to a flat expanse of open unoccupied land. The French shortened the word to "are" as a name for a measure of land equal to one hundred square meters.

Math Note (continued)

Perimeter has its origins in the Greek roots *peri* (around) and *metron* (measure). Peri shows up in other "around" words like periphery, the word the Greeks used for the circumference of a circle. The *pher* in the word means "to carry," and is the same as the ending in circumference. The first use in English seems to have been in the late 1400s.

Circumference has Latin roots uniting *circus,* the root of circle, with *ferre* which meant "to carry," thus literally "to carry around." The word is the Latin translation of the Greek word *periphereia* with the same meaning.

Parallel is derived from *para,* which is a root for "beside." Thus parallel refers to two lines that are beside each other.

Dimension is used in several different ways in math and science. When we talk about the dimension of a space we mean the number of coordinates needed to identify a point or location in that space. We also use the word to describe the units by which we measure objects. The origin of the word is indicative of this measurement theme. Dimension is a weathered and worn version of the union of dis (intense/strong) and meteri (measure), with a combined meaning of "measure carefully."

Modified from the website: http://www.geocities.com/Paris/Rue/1861/etyindex.html#a

Math Note
(Do NOT Distribute to the Students)

There are several methods available to you and your students to verify whether or not a rectangular base has been made. The following methods involve an understanding of the basic properties related to rectangles. Although your students are not expected to create rigorous geometric proofs, they are expected to perform physical demonstrations.

It is important to keep in mind the learning process during this activity. Students need time to explore creating the rectangle before they are asked to analyze its properties. Once they recognize the attributes that make their construction a rectangle, begin introducing the notion of justification to your students. What does it mean to prove something? Discuss ideas and encourage students to conjecture and test hypotheses. These necessary stages of learning provide the background for the justification of more formal mathematical statements.

Definition of a Rectangle

In Akiachak, unlike in other parts of southwest Alaska, there are lots of trees. This allows some leeway in designing a fish rack base. First one paces the length and the width of the rectangle, thus marking out an L shape on the ground (Fig. 6.5). Then one puts poles at the endpoints of L. Then one puts in the remaining poles using the poles already standing as a guide.

Fig. 6.5: Walking the "L" shape

PHYSICAL PROOF: Use the string to mark the width and check if the other width covers the same distance. Perform a similar operation for the length. Then estimate by sight, or with a book or some other object that has ninety-degree corners, to verify that the rectangle has at least two right angled corners.

Diagonal Theorem

When elder Henry Alakayak was asked how he would construct a fish rack if he had to begin in the middle, he explained the following method. He began by laying down four logs of equal length beginning from the center and toward where he envisioned the four corners of his rack to be (Fig. 6.6). To do this, he already had in the back of his mind some approximate measurements of the length and the width of

Math Note (continued)

the rack's rectangular base. Henry kept in mind the whole picture of a finished fish rack and marked each corner before he started digging.

Fig. 6.6: Measuring the diagonals with logs

PHYSICAL PROOF: Use string to verify that the diagonals of the rectangle are equal in length. The diagonals also need to bisect each other.

Perpendicular Bisector Theorem

PHYSICAL PROOF: Determine the midpoints of each side of the rectangle and use two pieces of string to connect each pair of opposite midpoints (Fig. 6.7). These pieces of string should cross perpendicularly, and you can use another object with right angles to verify this.

Fig. 6.7: Measuring bisectors with string

Math Note (continued)

Inscribed Rectangle Theorem

PHYSICAL PROOF: Someone stands in the center of the rectangle and holds a rope that stretches to the estimated corner of the rectangle. Someone else holds the other end of the rope taut and walks around the first person. The rope becomes the radius of a circle being traced on the ground that should intersect the rectangle at each corner (Fig. 6.8). This works because the four corners of a rectangle are always equidistant from its center. This proof is a dynamic demonstration because it brings together a relationship between two different geometric shapes.

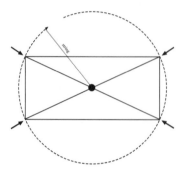

Fig. 6.8: A rectangle inscribed in a circle

Midpoint to Corner Theorem

PHYSICAL PROOF: Use a string to determine that the midpoint B of line AC is an equal distance from points D and F (Fig. 6.9). Likewise, verify that the midpoint E of line DF is an equal distance from points A and C. When the distances AE, CE, BF, and BD are all equal in length, the corners of a rectangle have been established.

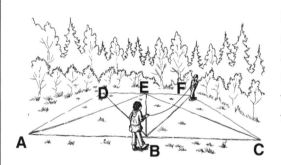

Fig. 6.9: Using string to determine the midpoint of the sides of a rectangle

Math Note (continued)

3-4-5 Right Triangle

In ancient Egypt there were people called "string stretchers." After the annual spring flooding of the Nile River, the land became covered with silt that enriched the soil for farming but often changed the shape of the land. The land needed to be divided so different families could cultivate it and so the Pharaoh could collect property taxes. Some historians believe that the roots of geometry came from the ancient Egyptians' measuring the amount of land washed away by the Nile in order to assess the taxes owed to the kingdom. The Egyptians were able to carry a straight line along the curving banks of the Nile River by utilizing several techniques including this one (Fig. 6.10). String stretchers tied twelve or thirteen equidistant knots in a rope (twelve knots if they used the end of the rope, and thirteen knots if they matched up knots). Through trial and error, they recognized that they could form right triangles with lengths of three, four, and five units.

Fig. 6.10: Egyptians finding a straight line on the curving banks of the Nile

PHYSICAL PROOF: Since your students have already created a 9 x 12 foot (2.7 x 3.7 m) rectangle, have them lay out a string along the diagonal and measure it. They should see that it is 15 feet long and that by dividing the rectangle along the diagonal they have formed two triangles with sides of 9 feet (2.7 m), 12 feet (3.7 m), and 15 feet (4.6 m). Ask students to take a piece of string and tie knots three feet apart until there are thirteen knots. Ask them to arrange the string into a triangle with sides that stretch three, four, and five knots. What is the measurement of the angle formed opposite the longest side? Any triangle that has lengths proportional to three, four, and five (the space between the knots) will be a right triangle. They should then lay the 3-4-5 knotted triangle over one of the triangles formed by dividing the rectangle along the diagonal. Is there a perfect match? What about the other triangle? Both should be 3-4-5 triangles, and thus the figure is a rectangle.

Historical Note

Ancient geometry was actually a collection of rule of thumb procedures derived through experimentation, observation of analogies, guessing, and occasional flashes of intuition. The word "geometry" comes from the Greek *geometrein* (*geo:* earth, and *metrein:* to measure). Geometry as a logical science is mostly a product of western civilization. Intuitive geometry, on the other hand, is universal.

The Yup'ik elders have developed their own rule of thumb procedures for constructing stable fish racks, using techniques of visualization, estimation, and measuring objects using parts of their bodies. Such information is still passed on orally from one generation to the next.

All ancient civilizations possessed knowledge of at the very least rudimentary mathematics. Some counted only one, two and many. Others developed methods of operating with larger numbers. Most cultures recognized the simplest geometric notions like line, circle, and angle. The concept of angle may have arisen from the observation of the angle formed by an individual's thigh and lower leg or forearm and upper arm because in most languages the word for the side of an angle is either the word for leg or the word for arm. The Yup'ik describe the sides of an angle using the word for leg [*iruq*] or the word for arm [*talliq*]. This relates to the discussion of body measure.

Mathematics took form as it was used to aid in the life of early civilizations. Dividing up land, counting food, constructing buildings (Fig. 6.11), and developing calendars are a few examples. The Babylonians were one of the first groups to contribute to the development of mathematics around 2000 B.C.E. Clay tablets were used to keep records. Applications of geometry and algebraic thinking are also evidenced in the ancient writings and architecture of both China and India.

Fig. 6.11: A Babylonian builder

Historical Note (continued)

The Greeks, however, were one of the first groups to systematize the body of mathematical knowledge. Beginning in 600 B.C.E. Thales of Milete insisted that geometric statements be established by deductive reasoning rather than by trial and error. Thales was a merchant in his youth, a statesman in mid-life, and a mathematician, astronomer and philosopher in his later years. He was also the teacher of Pythagoras, an influential force in the development of mathematics as we know it today. Pythagoras, who taught by word of mouth, not the written word, and his disciples believed that the study of mathematics and music elevated the soul closer to a union with pure spirituality. The Pythagoreans studied the properties of numbers. They were surprised to discover that irrational lengths existed, like the diagonal of a unit square being the square root of two. This marks a major break from earlier mathematics in that the irrationality of length could never have been discovered by physical measurements, which always included a small amount of experimental error.

Around 300 B.C.E., the Greek mathematician Euclid built on the work of his predecessors with the text known as *The Elements*. Euclid presented the first form of what we now call "pure mathematics." He began with certain axioms or assumptions, and built on them. The five undefined geometric terms that are the basis for defining all other geometric terms in Euclidian geometry are as follows: point, line, lie on (as in two points lie on a unique line), between (as in point C is between points A and B), and congruent (equal). No physical experiments were necessary to verify that statements were correct. Only the reasoning in the demonstrations needed to be checked. Mathematics was pure in that the work in *The Elements* included no practical applications. Euclid also did not use numbers, but proved geometric principles using lengths.

Euclidian geometry laid the foundation for western mathematical thought. Isaac Newton, who largely influenced our current understanding of the physical universe, used Euclidian geometry as a base. Connecting the development of mathematics to how we perceive and interact with the world today is essential to developing a holistic view of how things work in the universe.

The Yup'ik have also developed methods for using mathematics in their daily lives but have not needed to write it down in the form of pure mathematics. Their holistic view of the world is different from the westernized view. For example, rather than segmenting their environment (a common practice in Western civilization), they recognize and appreciate the connections between themselves and the workings of nature.

Activity 7:
Properties and Proof

Remember that constructing a rectangular base for the fish rack is important to the elders. The closer the base is to a rectangle the stronger and more stable the fish rack will be. This is a nice example of how in different contexts people will apply different standards for proof. For example, in building a fish rack the standard would mean constructing the object to stand a long time, be stable, hold the weight of the fish, etc. This knowledge implies a certain type and amount of experience such as a keen eye for visual measurement of length, knowledge of the weight of fish and the amount caught each year. The purpose of school mathematics is accuracy, precision and efficiency, which is different than that of constructing fish racks.

This activity contains three short explorations that deepen students ability to apply their newly learned knowledge of the properties of a rectangle to a different context. This time, rather than apply it to a practical exercise, building a fish rack base, they will apply it to more abstract exercises, providing proof of a rectangle on paper and relating the properties of a rectangle to other shapes. These extensions should help to consolidate their learning of the properties of a rectangle from the previous activities and strengthen their vocabulary before moving on to more difficult challenges. Understanding the properties of the various shapes will also aid in their modeling and building of fish racks in the concluding activities.

Goals
- To apply their knowledge of the properties of rectangles in a different context

- To determine an appropriate method of justification

Materials
- Worksheet, Properties Chart (one per pair of students)
- Worksheet, Vocabulary Cards (one per class or one per group)
- Worksheet, Vocabulary Cards (page 2) (one per class or one per group)
- Compasses (one per pair of students)
- Ruler (one per student)
- Protractor (one per pair of students)

Teacher Note

There are several ways in which your students may determine the center of their rectangle (Diagonal Theorem, Perpendicular Bisector Theorem, and Inscribed Rectangle Theorem). Invite your students to reason by counter example as well. For instance, what happens when the student has not found the absolute center? How do they know it is not the center? (See student work in Figs. 7.1, 7.2, and 7.3).

- Gumdrops and skewers (10 per pair of students): optional
- Student journals

Vocabulary

- Center—a point equally distant from all points on the circumference of a circle.
- Circle—the set of all points in a plane the same distance from the center (or a regular polygon with an infinite number of sides).
- Circumference—the distance around a circle.
- Counter example—an example that proves a statement is false.
- Diameter—a line segment that goes through the center of a circle and whose end points are on the circle.
- Equal—of the same quantity, size, or number.
- Inscribe—to draw within a figure so as to touch in as many places as possible.
- Property—a trait or characteristic of an object.
- Radius—a line segment with one endpoint at the center of a circle and the other endpoint on the circle.

Instructions

Introduce this activity by explaining to your students that today's activity is composed of three shorter explorations. These different explorations should aid in reviewing the properties learned in the previous activities, practicing the use of proof and counter examples, and allowing the newly gained knowledge to become internalized.

Exploration 1: Practice

1. Have students draw a rectangle in their journals, using a ruler or protractor. Tell them not to start at the center.

2. **Challenge.** Have students find the center of this rectangle by applying what they learned in Activity 6.

3. Have the students present their approach to the class.

> I learned that rectangles aren't so easy to make if you don't have anything to measure with. I also learned that the corners must be 90° or else it might be a diffrent shape. If you make a diagonal line from one side to the other and mark the middle you can find out if your rectangle is exact.

Fig. 7.1: An example of a student's understanding of using the diagonal theorem to find the center of a rectangle. The theorem states that if a rectangle has been created, then the intersection of the diagonals will mark the center of the shape

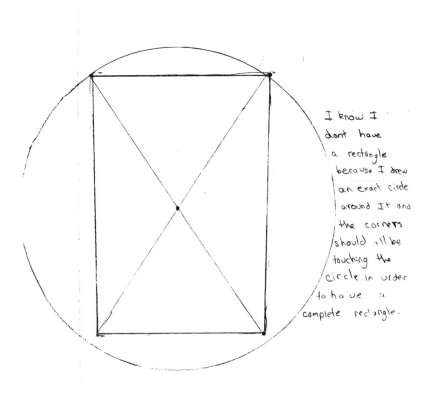

> I know I dont have a rectangle because I drew an exact circle around it and the corners should all be touching the circle in order to have a complete rectangle.

Fig. 7.2: A student's example of using the diagonal theorem to prove that the rectangular object is not truly a rectangle

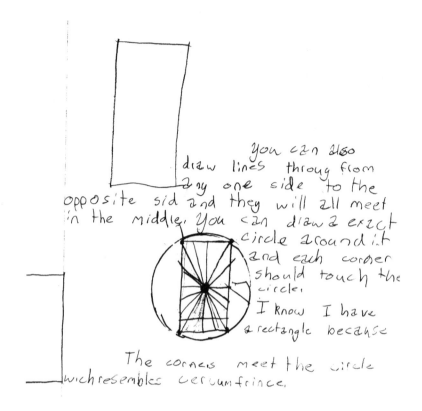

Fig. 7.3: Another example of the inscribed rectangle theorem. Here the student has included his own observations showing an additional concept that all the diameters of the circle will pass through the center point

Teacher Note

Answers may not neccesarily be yes or no. If students say 'sometimes' then have them explain. The point is to encourage creative and flexible thinking through a variety of cases before making conclusions. Encourage students to make counterarguments in their pairs to help decide what is really true.

Exploration 2: Proofs

1. Hand out the Properties Chart, one to each pair of students. Have various tools available for students to use: paper, pencils, protractors, rulers, gumdrops and skewers, etc.

2. **Demonstrate.** Ask students to provide a conjecture about the shape of a rectangle and the property of equal diagonals. (Students can either conjecture that a rectangle has equal diagonals or a rectangle does not have equal diagonals.) Demonstrate how to prove or disprove the conjecture by drawing a counterexample, using one of the theorems from the previous activity, or showing a counterexample with objects.

3. **Challenge.** Working in pairs, have the students proceed with the other blocks on the worksheet using any tools you set out for them. Have them make conjectures for each shape and property. After proving or disproving their conjectures have them mark all the properties that belong to each of the shapes.

4. Have each pair prove or make a convincing argument to another pair of students as to why they marked each case.

Properties

Shape	Equal Diagonals	Diagonals intersect in the middle	Diagonals bisect angles
Rectangle	yes	yes	no
Square	yes	yes	yes
Parallelogram	no	yes	no

Fig. 7.4: A key to the properties chart for the teacher. Notice that a counter-example should be shown for each block with a "no" in it

Exploration 3: Vocabulary Card Game

1. Hand out and have students cut apart the cards on the Vocabulary Card worksheets.

2. **Demonstrate.** Put the cards in a box or hat and mix them up. Randomly draw one card. Either act it out yourself or pick a student to act out the word on the card without talking. The other students should try to guess the word. The person who guessed the word correctly is the next one to act out a different card.

3. You may play this game in groups or as a whole class. If you have the students work in groups then copy enough pages so that each group has all the cards.

Teacher Note

There may be many words in this list that students have not had the chance to work with yet. Set aside the cards with vocabulary on them that should not be considered at this time. Or, if a card is selected and the student does not know its meaning, then have them replace the card and pick another one. Throughout the remainder of the module, revisit playing this game and include more of the cards as the students learn the new words.

Vocabulary Cards

point	parallelogram
line	rectangle
line segment	square
angle	circle
right angle	diameter
intersect	radius
perpendicular lines	circumference
plane	triangle
parallel lines	pentagon
bisector	hexagon
polygon	heptagon
regular polygon	octagon
congruent	diagonal
quadrilateral	inscribe

Vocabulary Cards (2)

estimate	kite
rhombus	unit
trapezoid	height
conjecture	derive
proof	constant
counter-example	maximum
theorem	minimum
perimeter	not equal
area	property
one-dimension	relationship
two-dimensions	90° angle
three-dimensions	opposite
measure	center
equal	

Properties Chart

Shape	Equal Diagonals	Diagonals intersect in the middle	Diagonals bisect angles
Rectangle			
Square			
Parallelogram			

Blackline Master

Activity 8:
Family Relations of Quadrilaterals

As students may have started realizing during the previous activities, if one or more properties are forgotten when trying to construct a rectangle then other shapes are possible. Also, two different shapes may share the same property such as equal diagonals or parallel sides. These similarities and differences arise because these shapes are part of a family, called the family of quadrilaterals.

The following explorations are designed to help students begin to better understand the relationships within this family. This understanding should translate into their knowledge of geometry as it provides a foundation for the understanding of shape based on properties rather than physical appearances. It should also aid them in beginning to think of mathematics more as relationships and patterns as opposed to right or wrong answers.

Goals

- To understand the properties of basic quadrilaterals

- To understand the relationships among members in the family of quadrilaterals

Materials

- Worksheet, Basic Quadrilaterals (one per student) made of note card or card stock paper (see Exploration 1)
- Worksheet, Shape Cards (one per group of three) made of note card or card stock paper (see Exploration 2)
- String
- Scissors
- Student journals

Vocabulary

- Angle—two line segments that have a common endpoint.
- Kite—a quadrilateral that has two pairs of sides the same length, but opposite sides are not the same lengths.

- Line segment—a figure that extends in one dimension and has two endpoints. A line segment is part of a line.
- Opposite—different in every way; exactly contrary.
- Polygon—a closed plane figure created by three or more lines segments such that each line segment intersects exactly two other segments at each endpoint and nowhere else.
- Quadrilateral—a polygon with four line segments and four angles.
- Regular polygon—a polygon that has all sides the same length and all angles the same.
- Rhombus—a parallelogram that has four sides of equal length.
- Trapezoid—a quadrilateral with exactly one pair of parallel sides.

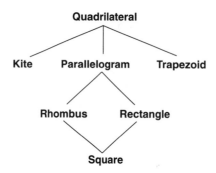

Fig. 8.1: Family Relations of Quadrilaterals

Instructions

Introduce today's activity by explaining to students that the following short explorations are designed to help them learn and internalize the properties of the different shapes they have been discussing in previous lessons. These explorations will help them understand how the shapes relate to each other and what is special about each shape.

Exploration 1: Visual Method

1. Demonstrate. Show students an example of the visual method by taking a piece of string and tying it in a knot to make a loop. Make a rectangle with your string and hands (Fig. 8.2). Show this shape to students. Then change the rectangle into a square by changing only the length of one set of parallel sides. Explain that you changed only one property—the length of one set of sides—and you were able to obtain a different shape.

2. Have students work in pairs. Hand out string to each pair of students. Hand out the Basic Quadrilaterals worksheet to each student for use as reference.

3. Have students make a loop in the string so that they can use their hands to make different shapes.

4. **Challenge.** Have students start with a square and then change the shape by changing only one angle or one length to get a new shape. Have them keep changing only one property at a time until they have discovered at least five shapes, all with four sides only (no circles, triangles, etc.). Have them record the progression of the shapes in their journals by recording the beginning and ending shapes each time.

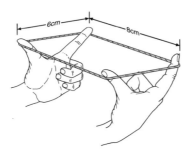

Fig. 8.2: Using string to form a rectangle

5. As students explore have them discuss, draw, and illustrate their family tree of quadrilaterals. An example of a family tree is shown in Fig. 8.1.

6. **Discuss.** Have students share their family trees and explain how shapes differ from one another, how many steps it took to change from one shape into another, and other properties they observed.

Exploration 2: Shape Card Game

1. **Demonstrate.** Pick 1-3 students to help demonstrate the game to the class. Pick one card from the set of six and say one property of that shape. Have the students guess the shape. Continue listing one property at a time until the shape is guessed.

2. Have students work in groups of three.

3. Hand out the Shape Cards to each group. Have them cut the cards apart and lay them upside down in a stack.

4. The first student picks a card and says a property. The other group members try to guess the shape.

5. The student who is describing continues to add description, one property at a time, until the other students have correctly identified the shape.

Teacher Note

For assistance in teaching the properties of various quadrilaterals consider what distinguishes one quadrilateral from another. What do the three shapes have in common?

Properties of Parallelograms

- The opposite sides are parallel.

- The opposite sides are congruent.

- The opposite angles are congruent.

- The diagonals bisect each other.

- Any pair of consecutive angles are supplementary.

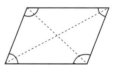

Properties of Rectangles

- All the properties of a parallelogram.

- All angles are right angles.

- The diagonals are congruent.

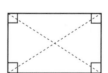

Properties of Squares

- All the properties of a rectangle.

- All the sides are congruent.

- The diagonals are perpendicular and they bisect each other.

- The diagonals divide the square into four isosceles right triangles.

6. **Optional.** Have each group play the game again using a slight varia-tion. Have students act out the shapes or properties instead of stating them verbally.

Exploration 3: Journal Writing

1. Have students list the following words in their journal: triangle, quad-rilateral, parallelogram, and polygon. Ask students to write their own definitions for each word in their journals.

2. Ask them to develop any "hints" that could be useful to help them in recognizing or remembering the definitions.

3. **Discuss.** Have students share their hints with the class.

Looking Ahead

At this point, the foundation for the fish rack has been established. In the next section, students will determine which properties of a fish rack are advantageous, such as stability and strength, and then construct either a real fish rack or a model that incorporates such properties. For the Yup'ik people, salmon was one of the most important food sources. It was plen-tiful and could last throughout the long winters if dried or smoked well. So it was absolutely critical that a fish rack be built to hold lots of fish and to dry it all quickly and thoroughly.

Basic Quadrilaterals

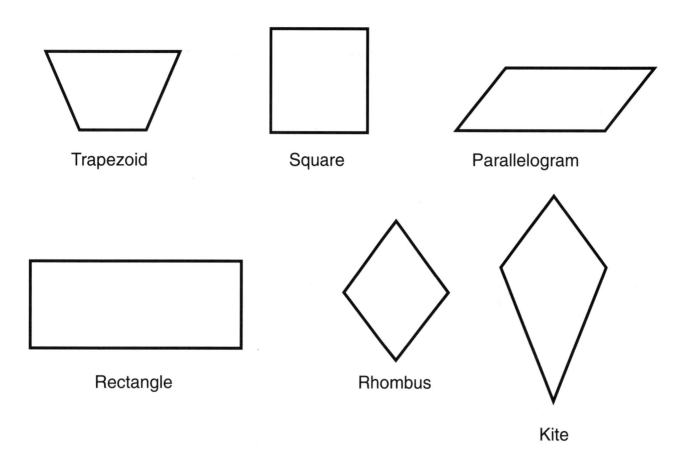

Trapezoid Square Parallelogram

Rectangle Rhombus

Kite

Shape Cards

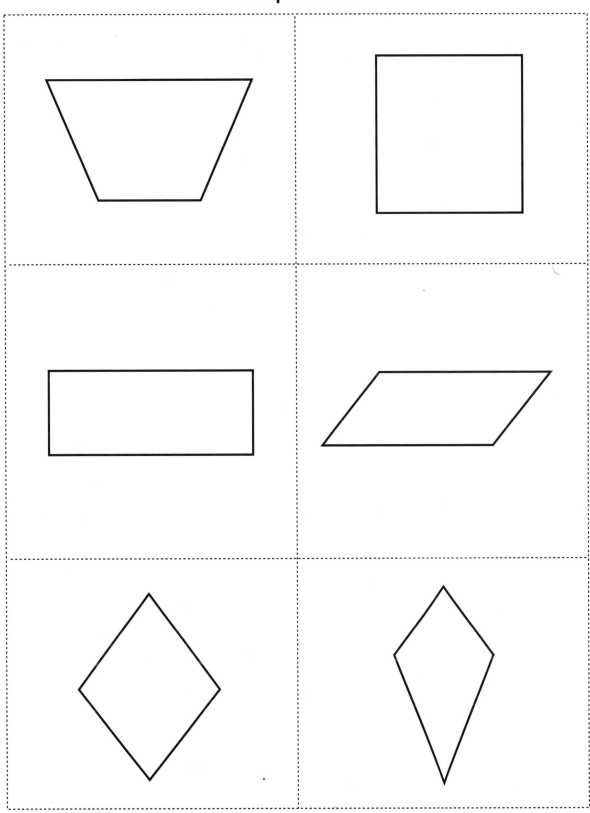

Blackline Master

Section 3

Designing a Fish Rack:
The Relationships between Perimeter, Area, Strength, and Shape

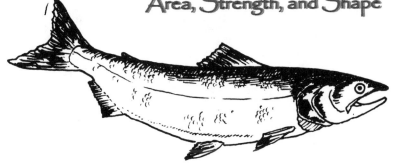

Activity 9:
Perimeter and Shape

Getting ready for seasonal activities is an essential part of Yup'ik life. Even in these modern times, Yup'ik people continue to prepare for the short, intense salmon fishing season. In Section 2, students were introduced to some of the general principles of building a fish rack. They investigated steps needed for constructing a rectangular base for their fish racks. The actual design and construction of a fish rack varies up and down the coast of Alaska. Varying cultural practices, environmental conditions, and personal preferences necessitate that even a simple structure, such as a fish rack, will differ from one village to the next. Sam Ivan, an elder from Akiak, explains: "In our area there are lots of trees. They have to cut a lot of trees to let the wind or breeze reach their fish racks. Because some of the soil is soft they have to put supports in between." In some coastal areas, there are few trees, and driftwood must be gathered and used for building a fish rack. These are just some of the considerations that the Yup'ik people need to take into account as they return to their summer fish camps.

As students begin to design and build a fish rack, they will be guided through activities that explore the relationship between the perimeter and the area of different shapes. Students will investigate a series of math-related activities dealing with maximizing the area of similar and different shapes when perimeter is held constant. Students also extend their explorations of area by perceiving the relationships between different shapes (for example, two trapezoids form a parallelogram), and by actually deriving area formulas for the various shapes.

The explorations of perimeter and area provide students with information that they will apply as they design their own model or life-size fish racks. Their design must be strong and big enough to hold the salmon they will "catch" later. The following activity is designed to help your students better understand the concept of perimeter and how it applies to several different shapes. This knowledge will provide them with more options as they prepare to design and build a fish rack.

Goals

• To use visualization and spatial reasoning to solve problems

• To estimate and predict solutions about the perimeter of various geometric shapes

- To understand that perimeter is a continuous measure or a one-dimensional length

Materials

- Worksheet, Map of Seagull Island (one map per student)
- Worksheet, Revised Map of Seagull Island (one map per student)
- Worksheet, Items at Fish Camp (one per student)
- String
- Scissors
- Rulers
- Protractors
- Glue or tape
- Spaghetti, dried
- Beans, dried, of various shapes and sizes
- Pennies
- Student journals

Fig. 9.1: Mrs. Charles and her fish rack at fish camp on Seagull Island

Vocabulary

- One-dimensional—having length only, no width and no height.
- Perimeter—the measure of the outer boundary of a figure or area.
- Two-dimensional—having length and width.
- Units—the smallest whole numbers of any quantity, amount, distance or measure.

Instructions

1. Hand out the Map of Seagull Island: one to each student. Have available spaghetti, beans, pennies, string, scissors, rulers, and protractors for each student. Explain to students that this is the island we'll use to set up our fish camp.

2. **Challenge.** Have the students determine the perimeter of Seagull Island as represented on the worksheet using any of the tools available. Students may talk to their neighbors about different strategies for accomplishing this task. Have them briefly describe their approach to solving this problem.

3. Have students share their strategies and measures with the class by using a transparency, showing their papers, or reconstructing their method.

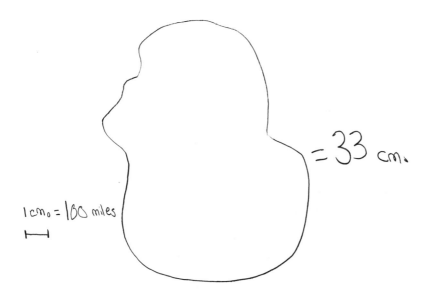

I found out what the distence around the Seagull Island. It is 33 cm.. I used a string that was longer then the full distence and I went around the outside and then I mesured it with a ruler. It's easyer for perimeter because it's just easeyer to find the length around the island. It's easyer to find to find the perimeter with a string. It's easyer to find the area with the grid.

Fig. 9.2: Student work explaining one method of measuring an irregular shape such as an island

Teacher Note

Based on what the students present, rephrase (either you or have another student) any comments that bring out the concept of perimeter as a continuous measure. If students used the string by laying it along the outline of the island, then stretch out the string in a straight line to show students a continuous one-dimensional measure (a measure with no breaks in it that follows a straight line).

4. Hand out the Revised Map of Seagull Island worksheet to each student. Ask them to conjecture (guess), how the perimeter of this island will relate to the perimeter they just calculated and why. Give them no more than five minutes to write their conjectures in their journals.

Teacher Note

The purpose of this activity is twofold. First, to impress on students that the perimeter is a 1D measure of a 2D object. Second, to show students they can't always use a formula but that there are good reasons for having formulas. The progression from the irregular to the regular shapes should aid in the evolution of the idea that there are easier ways of finding perimeter for regular shapes and thus using a formula is really taking a short cut. You may want to note for yourself when you see students using actual formulas, scaling strategies, and standard and nonstandard units of measure.

5. **Challenge.** Have students determine the perimeter of Seagull Island as newly represented on this second worksheet. Have them write their responses in their journals and briefly describe their approach to solving this problem and if it differed from their previous approach. (Note that if students created a grid on the original map they can use that map instead.)

6. Have students share any new approaches with the class and describe why they chose a different approach than previously used.

7. Hand out the Items at Fish Camp worksheet, one to each student.

8. Have students set up camp using either map of Seagull Island and the pieces to represent the fish rack, cabin, smokehouse, and cutting table. Have them label each object to show what they want it to represent on the island and glue or tape it on the island in an appropriate place.

9. **Challenge.** Have students measure the perimeter of each object using any tools available. Have them write their responses in their journals and briefly describe their approach to solving this problem and if it differed from their previous approaches. Encourage the students who finished quickly to justify the size of the island and the objects placed on it by choosing a scale they think is appropriate.

10. **Discuss.** Have students share any new approaches with the class and describe why they chose a different approach than previously used.

11. If you feel your students are having difficulty grasping that perimeter is a one-dimensional measure you may want to demonstrate the following activity. Stretch out a piece of string horizontally in the air or on a table or the board. Then bend it to form a rectangle without tying a knot. As the students watch you forming the rectangle ask them if the length of the string has changed. Have students discuss what they think is going on through student-to-student dialogue. This is an excellent opportunity for students to make convincing arguments about dimensionality and perimeter.

Student Responses

Here are some examples of students' responses from a 6th grade class in Fairbanks when asked, "Has the length of the string changed?" The results showed that although many students seemed to understand, about a third of the class thought the length or perimeter changed.

This group of responses shows student thinking around the idea that the perimeter is the same measurement as the straight line represented by the string. These students realized that although the shape changed, the measurement did not.

> *The length did not change. The shape changed. It's the same length of string but with a shape. All around the rectangle is still the same length as the string. No, the length is still the same. It was one dimension then two dimensions but it went back to one.*

> *No, you did not change it, because if you found the perimeter of the new shape it would be the same length if you measured like it as a string.*

> *No you didn't you just formed it in a different shape but it stayed the same length.*

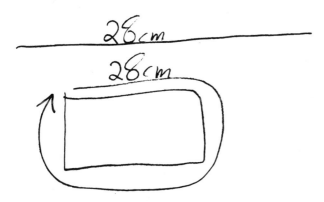

Fig. 9.3: An example of a student's answer with this picture for clarification

This group of responses shows student confusion around the idea of measurement and shape. Some refer to the language, using the term "length" specifically as opposed to a generic term for measurement. Others are confused with the visual aspect of the task. Yet other responses indicate students are not comprehending idea that perimeter is a measurement.

> *Yes, because if it were thirteen inches and then had to be split in four it would shrink.*

Yes, 'cause you made it shorter, Jerry. You also changed the shape. It was a line but then you made it a rectangle, dude.

Yes, it did change its shape. Long to short.

Yes, the length changed because you made it from a line with only length to a shape that had both length and width. It's like taking the lines length from it, you have to exchange some of the length to get some width which makes the length smaller.

12. In closing the activity, let students know that they will use their maps with the fish camp items in a future activity. Have them save the papers in a good spot or collect them.

Map of Seagull Island

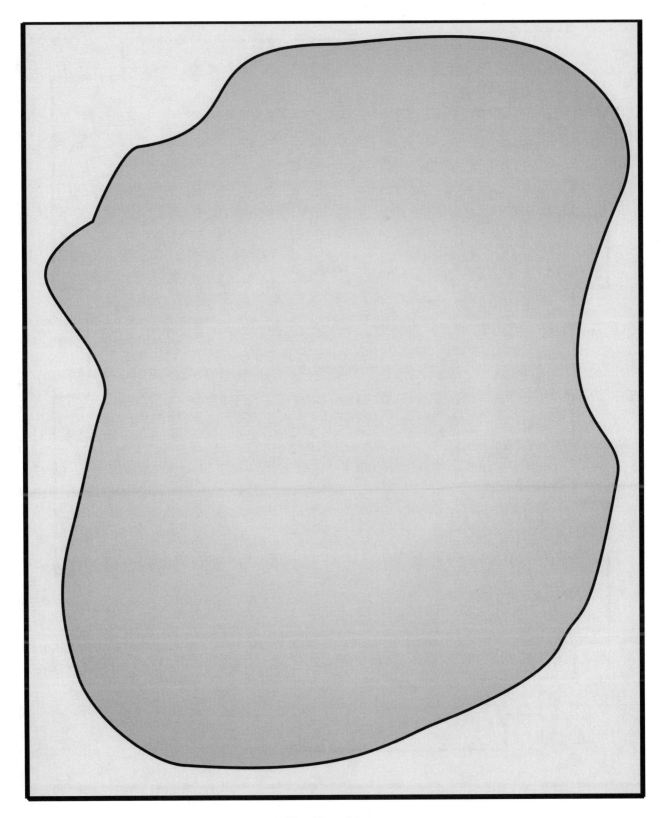

Revised Map of Seagull Island

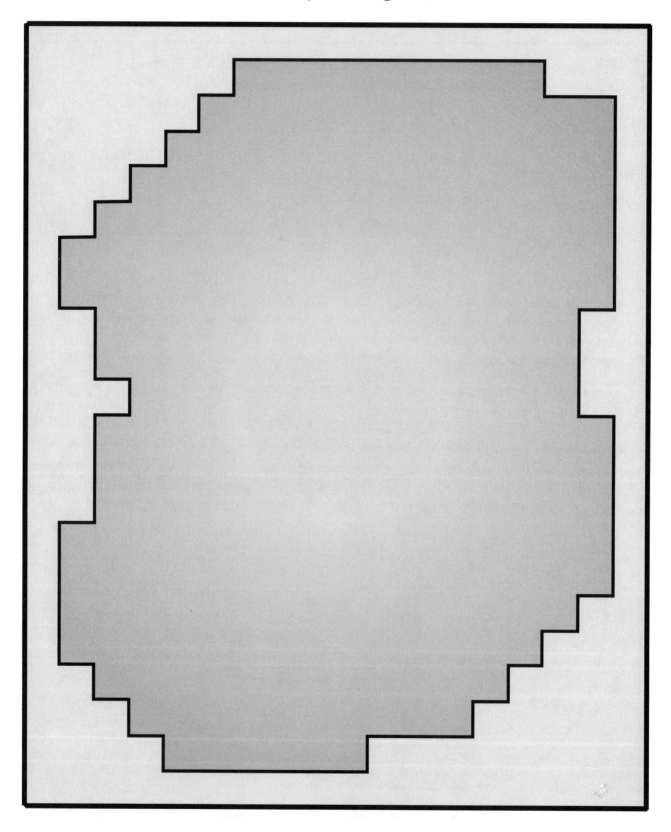

Items at Fish Camp

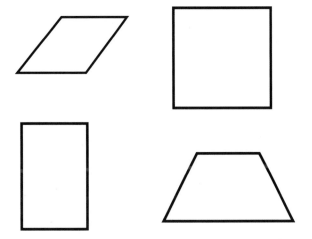

Activity 10:
Exploring Perimeter of Rectangles

Now that your students have a good feel for perimeter calculated for a variety of shapes, they will begin to focus more on rectangles only. As your students continue to design their fish rack models, they must consider a design that can hold many salmon and is strong enough to support these salmon. At the same time, the support beams cannot be so massive that their weight, combined with the drying salmon, is too heavy for the supporting poles. Finally, it should not be too difficult and time-consuming to build. For students to decide how big their model or real-life fish racks should be, they will need to explore how the shape of a fish rack determines its capacity to hold salmon. This activity begins the exploration by considering how the dimensions of a rectangle affect its perimeter.

Goals

- To develop the formula for the perimeter of a rectangle as the sum of the length of its sides

- To create a table to analyze different rectangles with the same perimeter

- To explore the relationship between a constant perimeter and different sized rectangles

Materials

- Transparency, Relationship of Perimeter and Dimensions of a Rectangle—Key
- Worksheet, Cm Graph Paper (one per student, found on page 200)
- Worksheet, Relationship of Perimeter and Dimensions of a Rectangle (one per student)
- Worksheet, Practice with Rectangles and Constant Perimeter (one per student)
- Worksheet, Extended Practice (two pages; one set per student)
- Rulers (one per student or pair)
- Ball of string, ruler, and scissors (for teacher only)
- Student journals

Duration

•   Two class periods.

Vocabulary

•   Constant—not changing; remaining the same.
•   Maximum—the greatest quantity, number, or degree possible or permissible.
•   Minimum—the smallest number, quantity, or degree.
•   Table—a compact, systematic list of related details, facts, figures, etc.

Instructions

1.   **Review.** Cut four pieces of string: two at 6 cm long and two at 8 cm long. On an overhead, arrange the strings into a rectangle. Tell the students the lengths as you place them on the overhead. Ask students, "What's the perimeter?" As they provide suggestions, rearrange the pieces to form a straight line. Have students express in their journals two different methods of calculating the perimeter of this rectangle.

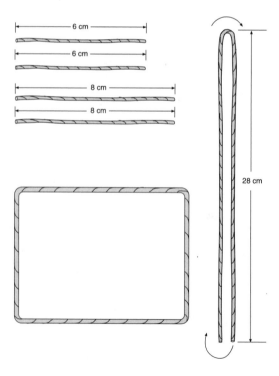

Fig. 10.1: The sum of the sides are its perimeter

2. **Demonstrate.** Take the ball of string and cut off one piece a little longer than 28 cm, then tie it into a loop that is as close as possible to 28 cm in circumference. Model different-sized rectangles by holding the string loop taut with your thumb and index finger of both hands (see Fig 10.2). By adjusting the distance between the thumb and index finger of each hand, you can change the dimensions of the rectangle.

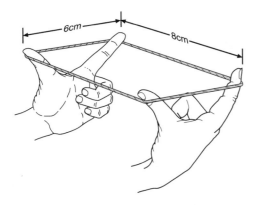

Fig. 10.2: The teacher can demonstrate the perimeter of the string

3. Have the students work in pairs. Hand out the Cm Graph Paper and rulers to each student.

4. **Challenge.** Working in pairs, have the students draw as many different rectangles they can think of with perimeter of 28 cm (keeping each side an integer value). Have them label the sides of each rectangle with its measurement. Tell students that they will need to save this work for later activities.

5. When students are ready to move on, hand out the worksheet Relationship of Perimeter and Dimensions of a Rectangle. Have students fill in the information using the rectangles they've just drawn. Allow groups to interact with each other to be sure that everyone finds all seven of the possible rectangles.

6. Place the transparency Relationship of Perimeter and Dimensions of a Rectangle—Key on the overhead or have students create the completed table on the board. Have students verify that all have the same results. Have several different students share their drawings for a particular rectangle especially for those with the same dimensions but oriented differently (vertically vs. horizontally).

Length (cm)	Width (cm)	Perimeter (cm)
1	13	28
2	12	28
3	11	28
4	10	28
5	9	28
6	8	28
7	7	28

Fig 10.3: An example of a filled-out table

7. **Discuss.** Have students discuss in small groups, and/or have students write in their journals.
   • How do we know we covered all possible rectangles?
   • Are two rectangles with the same dimensions but different orientations the same?
   • When the perimeter is held constant, what patterns do you see in the dimensions of the rectangle? Or when the perimeter is held constant, how does the length change when the width increases, decreases?
   • What formula can you use to calculate the perimeter of a rectangle?
   • What does this activity have to do with designing fish racks?

8. **Assess.** Hand out the worksheet Practice with Rectangles and Constant Perimeter, one to each student. Allow them twenty minutes or so to complete this worksheet. Encourage them to interact with other students and discuss in hopes that they will guide each other. Collect the papers and review to assess how much of your class is comfortable with the concept of perimeter.

9. **Optional.** The worksheet, Extended Practice is included for deeper practice in problem-solving strategies associated with perimeter and various shapes. You may want to hand this out for an in-class session where students can solve these problems using the problem-solving approach outlined in the introduction to the module. Or you may want to provide this as a homework assignment to use as further assessment. The solutions are provided below for the teacher.

   1. 4 cm
   2. 48 ft
   3. 36 in, P = 6 * s where s is the length of one side.
   4. 21 m, P = 3 * s where s is the length of one side.
   5. 32 cm, P = 8 * s where s is the length of one side.
   6. hexagon: 18 yd; triangle: 15 yd; square: 16 yd—hexagon has largest
   7. 28 ft, circumference

10. In closing, explain to students that they will need to save their drawings and charts of different rectangles with the same perimeter for later activities. Either collect the papers or have the students store them.

Teacher Note

Some students may have the numeric value correct while others have the spatial proportions correct and still others have coordinated the spatial and numeric values. "By learning how children think about measuring length and perimeter at different levels of development, teachers can attend more productively to children's needs to establish units, to relate space to their knowledge of addition and multiplication operations, to connect proportional reasoning to experiences with measurement and to the use of drawings that will support connections and coordination of units and collections of units of length" (p. 47). (*Children's Developing Knowledge of Perimeter Measurement in Elementary, Middle, and High School.* Jeffrey E. Barrett, Douglas H. Clements, David Klanderman, Sarah-Jean Pennisi, Mokaeane V. Polaki. Paper presented at the Annual Meeting of the American Educational Research Association, Seattle, WA; April 10–14, 2001.)

Relationship of Perimeter and Dimensions of a Rectangle—Key

Length (cm)	Width (cm)	Perimeter (cm)
1	13	28
2	12	28
3	11	28
4	10	28
5	9	28
6	8	28
7	7	28

Relationship of Perimeter and Dimensions of a Rectangle

Length (cm)	Width (cm)	Perimeter (cm)
1		
2		
3		
4		
5		
6		
7		

Practice with Rectangles and Constant Perimeter

Assume that you have a perimeter of 32 inches. In the space provided below draw four different rectangles (approximately to scale) that have a perimeter of 32 inches. Label all dimensions.

A. Rectangle #1

B. Rectangle #2

C. Rectangle #3

D. Rectangle #4

Extended Practice

Show, draw or explain your process for solving each problem.

1. The perimeter of a square is 16 cm. What is the length of a side?

perimeter = 16

2. If the length of one side of a rectangle is 16 ft and the length of another side is 8 ft, what is the perimeter?

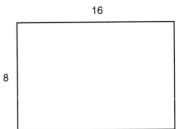

3. If one side of a regular hexagon is 6 inches, then what is the perimeter? What is the formula for the perimeter of a hexagon?

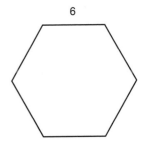

4. An equilateral triangle has one side of 7 meters. What is the perimeter? What is the formula for the perimeter of a triangle?

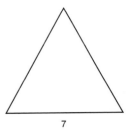

Extended Practice (continued)

5. If one side of a regular octagon is 4 cm, then what is its perimeter? Write a formula for the perimeter of an octagon.

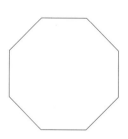

6. Which shape would have the largest perimeter: a hexagon with a side of 3 yds, an equilateral triangle with a side of 5 yds, or a square with a side of 4 yds?

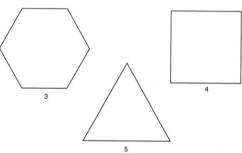

7. Take a rectangle with a perimeter of 28 ft, then push out its sides so that the shape turns into a circle. What is the perimeter of this circle? What is another word for *perimeter* of a circle?

Activity 11:
Measuring Area

Previously in this module students have physically explored the properties of a rectangle, investigated and identified physical proofs, and explored dynamic aspects of perimeter. These explorations were culturally connected to the design and building of a rectangular structure such as a fish rack. In the next few lessons, students will be exploring the concept of area with an emphasis on rectangles, squares and other quadrilaterals—such as parallelograms and trapezoids. The cultural connection to fish racks is two-fold. First, the shape of a fish rack tends to be rectangular because it is a convenient design for hanging up fish and taking them down. Second, viewing the space used by fish racks or poles can be perceived as a rectangular plane. This space for drying can be viewed as two dimensions, having length and width. Filling this space with salmon can be perceived as area.

As students explore area in the next set of lessons they will learn to connect visual and spatial notions of perimeter and area to numerical notions. These activities will assist them in coordinating spatial and numerical understandings. Further, students will explore and learn to derive area formulas of other quadrilaterals from the area of a rectangle. Students will also practice calculating area. This all begins with students creating their own units of measure for the area of Seagull Island and the fish camp items used in Activity 9.

Goals

- To establish and explain how to create a unit of measure for a rectangle

- To solve a problem (devising units of measure), mathematically communicate the process and the solution

Materials

- Completed items from Activity 9 (two maps of Seagull Island with one including fish camp items attached)
- String
- Scissors
- Rulers
- Protractors
- Glue or tape
- Spaghetti, dried

Math Note

Whenever there is a closed, two-dimensional shape then two properties exist automatically. The shape has an outside path that can be measured as a length (one-dimensional measure), this is called the perimeter. Using the string to measure perimeter in Activity 9 should have helped students understand that the measure itself is one-dimensional. Second, the shape has a space inside called the area that can be measured differently by using two-dimensional objects or those with both length and width. These two measurements, perimeter and area, co-exist for any closed two-dimensional shape. Students often confuse these concepts since you can not have one without the other.

This applies to closed three-dimensional shapes as well. The outside now consists of many areas and is called surface area. The inside is measured differently, usually thought of as consisting of centimeter-cubes, and is called volume. By convention, perimeter and area are meaningless for any closed three-dimensional shape and only the terms surface area and volume are used.

- Beans, dried, of various shapes and sizes
- Pennies
- Student journals

Vocabulary

- Area—the measure of a bounded region on a plane.
- Three-dimensional—having length, width, and height.

Instructions

1. Hand out or ask students to get out their completed work from Activity 9: two maps of Seagull Island with one including fish camp items attached. Have available spaghetti, beans, pennies, string, scissors, rulers, and protractors for each student. Explain to students that we now want to know the area of our island and fish camp items.

2. **Challenge.** Have the students determine the area of Seagull Island as represented on the worksheet (use either map) using any of the tools available. Students may talk to their neighbors about different strategies for accomplishing this task. Have them write their responses in their journals and briefly describe their approach to solving this problem. See the Teacher Note on page 139 concerning the use of a repeated core unit. Discussion should focus around this idea.

3. Have students share their strategies and measures with the class. It is likely that several different numbers may arise as answers for the area of the island because students may have used different units or materials. Have students discuss and justify the different responses. Encourage them to talk in groups and then among the entire class about how different numbers can measure the same space. Motivate them to consider the various units and tools used to measure area and how they relate to each other.

4. **Challenge.** Have students determine the area of each of the fish camp items attached to the map using any tools available. Have them write their responses in their journals and briefly describe their approach to solving this problem and if it differed from their previous approach to calculating area.

Teacher Note

The purpose of this activity is to show that a "unit" of measure must be consistently applied and all units must be equal. As students work through this exercise they will progress from illustration A, to B, to C, to D. Your students may end up making units of measure that are uneven as illustrated in Figure C. If so have each group continue to work on this problem until they have solved it, that is, until all units are equal.

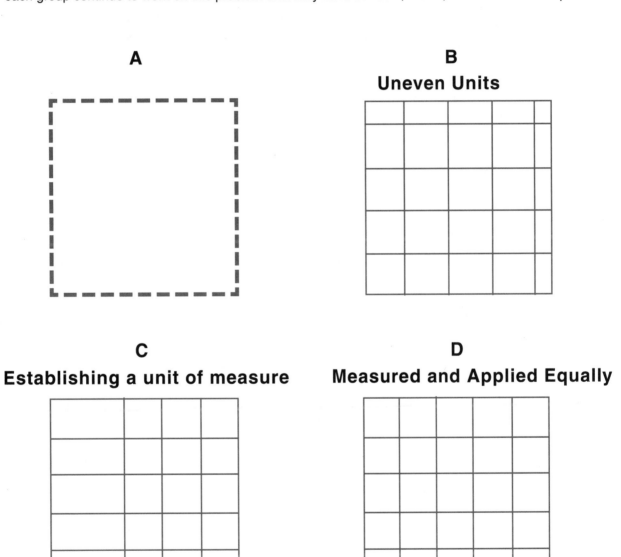

A

B
Uneven Units

C
Establishing a unit of measure

D
Measured and Applied Equally

5. **Discuss.** Have students compare methods among themselves for about five minutes. Then have students share any new approaches with the class and describe why they chose a different approach than previously used. Be sure to point out or ask students' opinions on the usefulness and disadvantages of the different approaches to calculating area.

Additional resources relating to students' creation of two-dimensional units can be found at http://www.kidsdigreed.com/games.asp.

Activity 12:
Investigating the Relationship of Perimeter and Area of Rectangles

Now that students have determined methods for calculating perimeter and area for various shapes, in this exercise they will further explore the relationship between perimeter and area of rectangles. Students will begin to see that using the same length of material (perimeter), they can design fish racks to maximize the usable space (area) for hanging and drying salmon.

Goals

- To analyze the relationship between the perimeter and area of a rectangle

- To create a table and a graph showing this relationship

Materials

- Completed worksheet of all rectangles with perimeter of 28 cm from Activity 10
- Transparency, Rectangular Fish Racks with Perimeter of 28 Units
- Transparency, Relationship of Area and Dimensions of a Rectangle— Key
- Transparency, Graph of Length and Width of a Rectangle
- Transparency, Graph of Area and Length of a Rectangle—Key
- Worksheet, Cm Graph Paper (one per pair of students; found on page 200)
- Worksheet, Relationship of Area and Dimensions of a Rectangle
- Worksheet, Graph of Area and Length of a Rectangle (optional)
- Rulers (one per pair of students)
- Student journals

Duration

- Two to three class periods.

Vocabulary

- Graph—a diagram, as a curve, broken line, series of bars, etc.

- Horizontal axis (or *x*-axis)—parallel to the plane of the horizon; not vertical.
- Ordered pair—a pair of numbers used to locate a point on a graph with the first number showing the value on the horizontal axis and the second number showing the value on the vertical axis.
- Scale—ratio between the dimensions of a representation and those of an object.
- Vertical axis (or *y*-axis)—that which is perpendicular to the horizontal axis.

Instructions

1. Introduce today's activity by sharing a conjecture. Write the following on the board. Conjecture: The perimeters of different rectangles are the same, so they will hold the same number of fish (meaning that they will have the same area).

2. Show your students the transparency Rectangular Fish Racks with Perimeter of 28 Units. Explain that each line represents a pole on the fish rack and after studying these different fish racks, you believe that your conjecture is true.

3. **Challenge.** Have students prove or disprove the conjecture. If they agree with the conjecture, then they must show it's true. If they disagree, they must provide a counter example.

4. **Discuss.** Have students share their results—both those for and against the conjecture—with the class. Encourage students to discuss opposing views.

5. To have the students further analyze this conjecture, have them take out their completed worksheet of all rectangles with perimeter of 28 cm from Activity 10. Working in pairs, have students label the length and width of each rectangle if there are no previous labels.

Teacher Note

Previously, students were challenged to divide up 28 cm in order to form two equal sides of a rectangle. As students view the area of rectangles based on the construction of every possible rectangle with a perimeter of 28 cm, the visual effect is dramatic. Students can see the difference between a 1 cm x 13 cm rectangle, and a 2 cm x 12 cm rectangle. The width increases by one, as the length decreases by one, and the area increases. This process continues, until they reach a 7 cm x 7 cm rectangle or square. As they continue increasing the width to 8 cm and above, students should notice that even though the width of each rectangle is still increasing by one, and the length decreasing by one, the area is now decreasing.

6. Ask students to make a conjecture about which fish rack design they believe would hold the most salmon, draw it in their journals and briefly explain their reasoning.

7. Hand out the Relationship of Area and Dimensions of a Rectangle worksheet to each pair and have students fill in the answers.

Perimeter (cm)	Width (cm)	Length (cm)	Area (cm²)
28	1	13	13
28	2	12	24
28	3	11	33
28	4	10	40
28	5	9	45
28	6	8	48
28	7	7	49
28	8	6	48
28	9	5	45
28	10	4	40
28	11	3	44
28	12	2	24
28	13	1	13

Fig. 12.1: Relationship of area and dimensions of a rectangle

8. **Discuss.** Ask students to explain their findings to the class and how they arrived at their solutions. If necessary, use the transparency of the Relationship of Area and Dimensions of a Rectangle—Key to enhance the discussion. The ideas that the closer the rectangle becomes to a square, the bigger the area and that the length and width act opposite of each other should come out.

This may be a good stopping point for the day. If you choose to end the activity here, then ask the students to store their charts for tomorrow's lesson and begin tomorrow with step 9.

Teacher Note (continued)

When students count the squares and fill in the table, they should also start to notice numerical patterns. For instance, they may recognize that there is more than one rectangle with the same area. A rectangle with an area of 45 cm² exists when the width is 5 cm and the length 9 cm, and also when the width is 9 cm and the length 5 cm. Students who already know multiplication may notice that both 5 x 9 = 45 and 9 x 5 = 45. For students who do not yet know multiplication, the concept that five rows of nine squares and nine rows of five squares have the same area can introduce multiplication in a tangible way.

9. **Demonstrate.** Use the transparency Graph of Length and Width of a Rectangle to model how to transfer values from the table to a chart showing the relationship between length and width. The ideas of using an ordered pair, setting up the chart with *x*- and *y*-axes, labeling the axes, and determining the best scale for both axes should be discussed through the modeling.

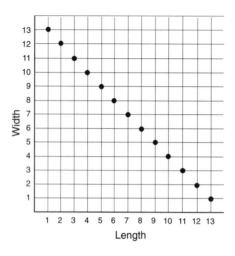

Fig. 12.2: Graph of length and width of a rectangle

10. Once the graph of length versus width is complete, have the students practice reading the graph. The following sample questions are given as a guide, but you should ask other relevant questions to allow for plenty of practice.
   - Given a length, can you draw the rectangle? For example, if the length is six units, draw the rectangle. (Answer: 6 units x 8 units rectangle.)
   - Given a width, can you tell me the length? For example, if the width is ten units, what is the length? (Answer: 4 units.)
   - Given a point on the graph, can you tell me the dimensions of the rectangle? For example, what is the rectangle represented by the point (1, 13)? (Answer: length of 1 unit and width of 13 units.)
   - What is the one property that allows us to consider the relationship here? (Answer: Perimeter unchanging: always 28 units.)

You may want the students to practice creating the same graph on their own using the completed one as a model.

This may be a good stopping point for the day. If you choose to end the activity here, then ask the students to store their graphs for tomorrow's lesson and begin tomorrow with step 11.

11. **Challenge.** Have students work in pairs. Have them create a graph or chart showing the relationship between the length and the area. If you find the students need more help you may want to continue modeling or hand out the worksheet Graph of Area and Length of a Rectangle to each pair of students (notice that the axes are already defined and labeled).

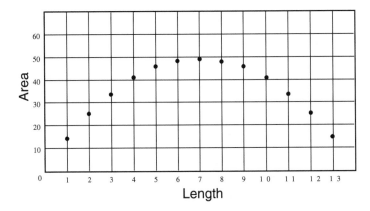

Fig. 12.3: Graph of rectangle's length to its area

12. **Discuss.** Have students share their results with the class. Allow them to discuss how the picture relates to the values; other relationships that can be seen; and how this graph can be used in deciding how to build the best fish rack. If necessary, use the transparency Graph of Area and Length of a Rectangle to enhance the discussion. Have students practice reading the graph by asking similar questions as those suggested in step 10.

Rectangular Fish Racks with Perimeter of 28 Units

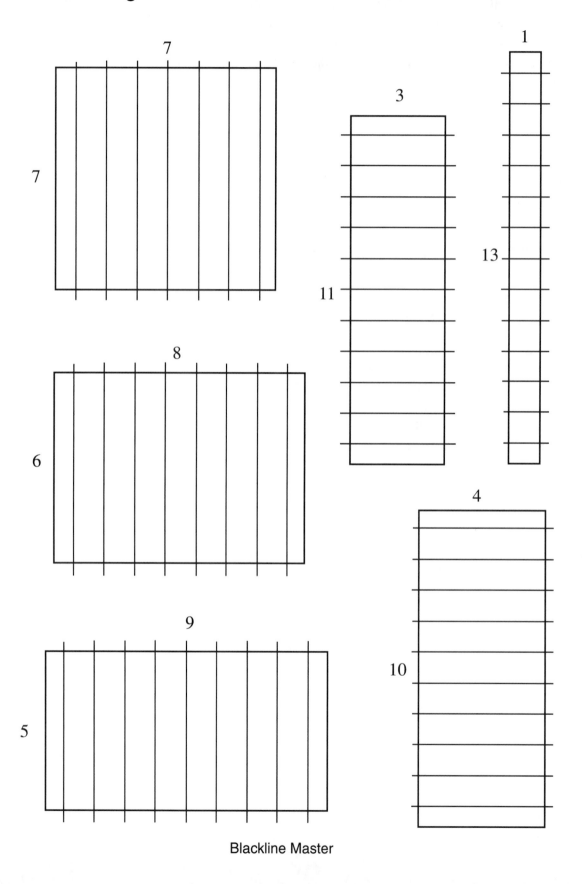

Relationship of Area and Dimensions of a Rectangle—Key

Perimeter (cm)	Width (cm)	Length (cm)	Area (cm^2)
28	1	13	13
28	2	12	24
28	3	11	33
28	4	10	40
28	5	9	45
28	6	8	48
28	7	7	49
28	8	6	48
28	9	5	45
28	10	4	40
28	11	3	44
28	12	2	24
28	13	1	13

Graph of Length and Width of a Rectangle

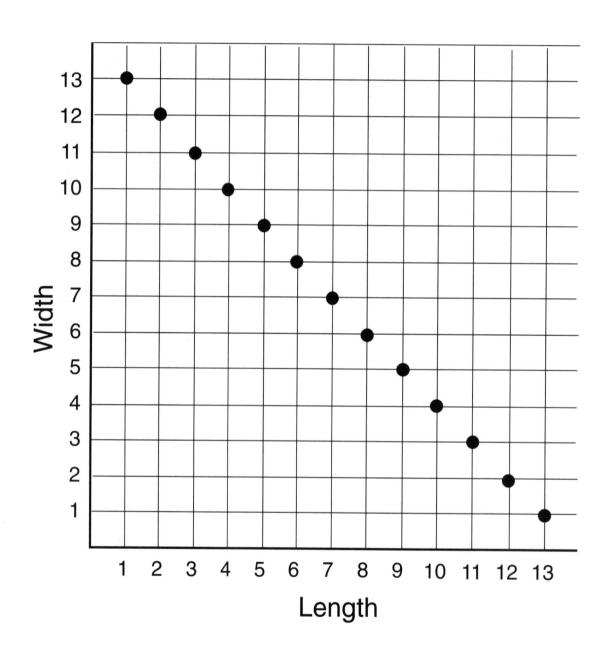

Graph of Area and Length of a Rectangle—Key

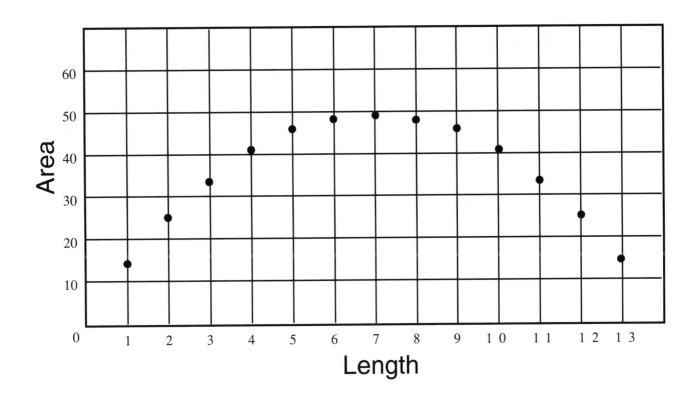

Relationship of Area and Dimensions of a Rectangle

Perimeter (cm)	Width (cm)	Length (cm)	Area (cm^2)
28			
28			
28			
28			
28			
28			
28			
28			
28			
28			
28			
28			
28			

Graph of Area and Length of a Rectangle

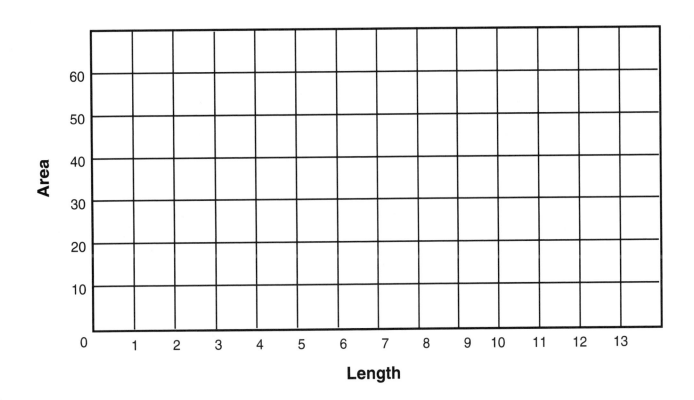

Activity 13:
Area of Different Shapes

Building on the previous activities of perimeter and area, students will apply their knowledge to shapes other than rectangles. They will predict and explore which geometric shape has the greatest area when the perimeter is held constant.

Most fish racks are rectangular because the Yup'ik have found this to be the easiest shape to build with the materials they generally have on hand, such as spruce trees or driftwood. Knowledge about building strong and stable fish racks is passed on by the Yup'ik elders, who learned it from their elders. Students will learn some of this knowledge as they explore why most fish racks are rectangular, not triangular or circular.

Goals

- To analyze the areas of different shapes when the perimeter is held constant

- To develop different methods for finding area, such as counting squares and recognizing patterns

- To use geometric shapes to examine changes in both real (fish rack) and abstract (paper) contexts

Materials

- Transparency, Geometric Shapes with Constant Perimeter
- Worksheet, Cm Graph Paper (four sheets per pair of students; found on page 200)
- String (one to two foot [0.3 to 0.6 m] length per group of students)
- Scissors (one per group of students)
- Push pins (four per group of students)
- Piece of cardboard (one per group of students)
- Compass (one per group of students)
- Ruler (one per pair of students)
- Four 10-inch (25 cm) skewers (for teacher demonstration)
- Four gumdrops (for teacher demonstration)
- 15 to 20 foot (4.6 to 6 m) length of rope, for class demonstration
- Student journals

Duration

- One to two class periods.

Vocabulary

- Triangle—a three-sided polygon.

Instructions

1. Introduce today's activity by telling this short story.

   One day rectangle, square, circle, and triangle ran into each other, each boasted that it had special properties. The ruler found them bickering and bragging and asked them, "Which one of you will cover the greatest area if your perimeter is held constant?" The figures argued, each claimed that it covered the greatest area. Let's find out which shape with a perimeter of 28 cm has the greatest area.

2. Show the transparency Geometric Shapes with Constant Perimeter. Have students write in their journals their conjecture as to which object has the greatest area and why.

Fig. 13.1: Geometric shapes with constant perimeter

3. **Demonstrate.** Model for the students how to create the various shapes with constant perimeter using a rectangle. Form a loop of string 28 cm long. Place cardboard under a piece of graph paper. Create a rectangle using the string and use pins to hold the string on the graph paper without changing shape. Trace the shape onto the graph paper using a ruler to make the sides straight.

4. Have the students work in groups of three. Hand out string, scissors, graph paper, cardboard, push pins, rulers, and compasses. Have them draw four shapes—a circle, square, rectangle, and triangle—onto the graph paper, each with a perimeter of 28 cm.

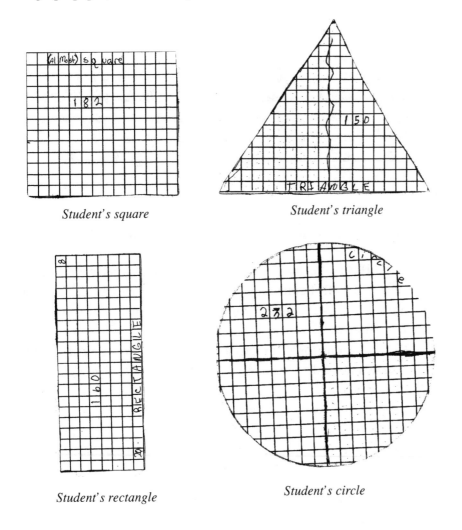

Student's square

Student's triangle

Student's rectangle

Student's circle

Fig. 13.2: Students' shapes: In this exercise, students were striving for a perimeter of 56 cm.

Math Note

In this section, students are solving classic mathematics and real world problems. Students have been challenged to explore problems associated with area and perimeter when perimeter is held constant. Typically, students engage in procedural routines when learning about perimeter and area. However, the non-intuitive and novel problems in this activity challenge students to think mathematically and to come to a more fundamental understanding of perimeter and area.

Traditionally when students learn about area when perimeter is held constant, they are asked to determine the dimensions of a fence that has the greatest area. This problem appears again later in mathematics as students learn how to apply the quadratic formula ($ax^2 + bx + c = d$) and in calculus many problems focus on finding the maximum or minimum point of a function or area under a curve.

5. **Challenge.** Have students determine the area inside each shape by whichever method they want: counting the squares, visually estimating, or using mathematical formulas. Remind them they are doing this in order to prove or disprove their conjectures from step 2.

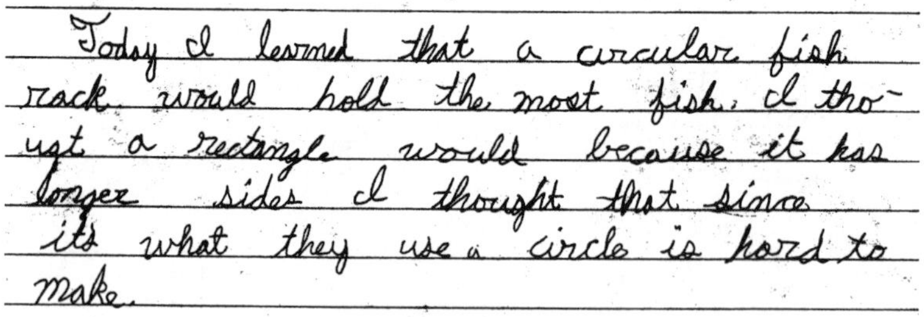

> Today I learned that a circular fish rack would hold the most fish. I thought a rectangle would because it has longer sides I thought that since its what they use a circle is hard to make.

Fig. 13.3: One student's conclusion about which shaped fish rack would hold the most fish and why it wouldn't be a good choice to use

6. **Discuss.** Have students discuss their methods and answers in class; however, they all should conclude that the circle possesses the greatest area. If necessary, to encourage further mathematical explorations, pose the following questions:
   - Has any group found a shortcut to counting the number of squares?
   - Is calculating the area of a circle different than calculating that of a rectangle?
   - How did you calculate the area of a circle?
   - Can you discover a formula for the area of a square or a rectangle?
   - How is the area of the triangle related to the area of the rectangle?

Exploration 1: Culminating Conjecture

1. Write the following conjecture on the board. Mrs. X says that if a rectangle and a triangle have the same perimeter then the area of the rectangle is bigger than the area of the triangle.

2. **Challenge.** Have students prove or disprove the conjecture.

3. **Discuss.** Have students share their reasoning and conclusions with the class. Expect uncertainty and differences of opinion while students are sharing. Encourage students to discuss in more depth as this is a culminating exploration that pulls together many of the aspects of properties, conjecture, and proof. Encourage students to share if their various forms of proof are sufficient to convince their peers.

Exploration 2: Class Demonstration

1. Because of the counterintuitive nature of different shapes having different areas when perimeter is held constant, have the students participate in the following class demonstration. Use a 15 to 20 foot (4.5 to 6 m) long rope. Tie the ends together to form a loop. Have yourself and one student each hold one point keeping the rope taut. This will produce a line. Invite a third student to pick a point toward the middle of the rope and pull the rope, so that each person now is holding approximately equal lengths, forming a triangle. Add another student, and follow this procedure to form a quadrilateral. Keep doing this, until every student in the class is holding and pulling a point on the rope. Have the students pay attention to the changing shapes and the increasing space formed within the loop. The students should be able to see that each additional side and angle added to the loop increasingly transforms the shape, until it approximates a circle (See Fig. 13.4).

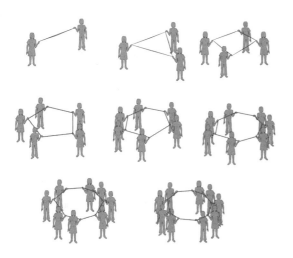

Fig. 13.4: Using a rope to transition from a line to a circle

2. Ask the class: "Although the circular shaped fish rack would hold the most salmon, why wouldn't it be a good choice?" Students should state that it is a lot of work to build, difficult to make with materials such as logs, and does not allow for easy access to the inner racks, etc. Ask: "What shape(s) would make a more practical fish rack?"

Math Note

How to determine the maximum or minimum area of a figure, when the perimeter is held constant, is sometimes a counterintuitive process. Many individuals assume that when the perimeter is held constant, the area will also be held constant. Through the series of activities in this problem, students are provided several opportunities to "see for themselves" what happens to the area inside a figure of constant perimeter as it is moved into different shapes. The rope demonstration is effective because as the number of people holding the rope increases, the space inside the rope increases, even though the length of the rope has not changed.

Exploration 3: Parallelograms

1. **Demonstrate.** Connect four 10-inch (25 cm) skewers using gumdrops to make a square. As you slowly push the opposite corners of the square toward each other, creating a parallelogram, ask your students for conjectures on what is happening to the area (stays the same, changes, increases, decreases).

2. Have students write their conjectures in their journals.

3. Have students prove or disprove their conjectures.

4. Have students present their conjectures, proofs, and results to the class.

*Fig. 13.5: Gumdrop-skewer square converted to
parallelogram*

Geometric Shapes with Constant Perimeter

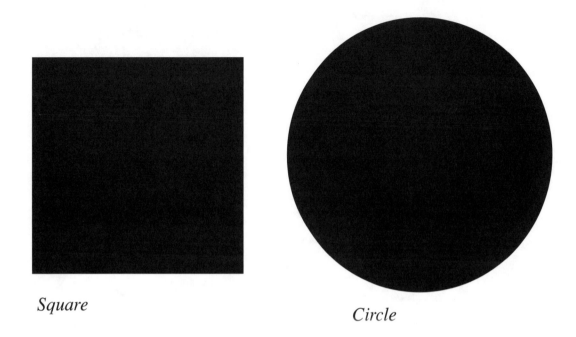

Square

Circle

Rectangle

Triangle

Activity 14:
Deriving Area Formulas

In the following exercises, students derive the formula for the area of two shapes: a parallelogram and a triangle. To do so, they will need to convert the given shapes into other shapes whose formulas for area are already known (such as a rectangle). Students should work in pairs with ample time to discover the solutions on their own.

In the Practice Activity at the end of this activity, students have a chance to pull together the knowledge gathered throughout the activities on perimeter and area before moving on to the final stage of the module: building the fish racks. The practice can be used as a study tool or an assessment for individuals, pairs, or small groups. It contains some questions that focus on shapes not discussed in this activity. Encourage students to use the Problem-Solving Approach discussed on page 6 in the Introduction to this module. The answer key can be found on page 174. Lastly, an optional transparency How to Derive the Area of a Trapezoid is included on page 169 as an additional challenge.

Goals

- To derive the formulas for area of a parallelogram and triangle

- To use area formulas for other shapes in deriving area formulas for more complicated shapes

Materials

- Transparency, How to Derive the Area of a Parallelogram
- Transparency, How to Derive the Area of a Triangle
- Transparency, How to Derive the Area of a Trapezoid (optional)
- Worksheet, Cm Graph Paper (four sheets per pair of students; found on page 200)
- Worksheet, Three Different Sized Triangles (one per pair of students)
- Worksheet, Practice Activity (one per student)
- Scissors (one per pair of students)
- Ruler (one per pair of students)
- Student journals

Vocabulary

- Derive—to trace from or to a source; deduce or infer.

- Height of a parallelogram—the perpendicular distance between the base and the opposite side.
- Height of a triangle—the perpendicular distance from one side to the opposite angle.
- Perpendicular lines—lines that intersect to form ninety-degree angles, or right angles.

Instructions

Explain to students that today's activity will use their skills and knowledge developed throughout the module to derive the area formulas for parallelograms and triangles.

Exploration 1: Parallelogram

1. Hand out scissors, ruler, and four copies of the Cm Graph Paper to each pair of students.

2. **Challenge.** Have students cut out a parallelogram from the graph paper. Encourage them to cut it in pieces in order to rearrange it into an easier shape. Allow the students about ten minutes to determine the area formula of the parallelogram. Tell the students they can use any method and any tools available.

    Solution: Cut the parallelogram along the height, forming two pieces. Rearrange the pieces so that they make a rectangle. Students can copy the newly-formed rectangle onto the graph paper and calculate the area of the new rectangle by counting the squares of the graph paper or by using a formula. The area of the new rectangle (b x h) is the area of the parallelogram.

3. **Discuss.** Have several students show their methods on the board or on an overhead for determining the area of the parallelogram.

4. If students are unable to see the relationship between a rectangle and a parallelogram, share the transparency How to Derive the Area of a Parallelogram (Fig. 14.1). Have students describe how the height of the parallelogram differs from the height of a rectangle.

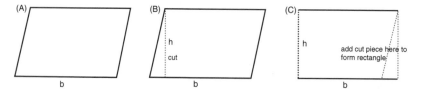

Area of a parallelogram = b x h
Area of a rectangle = b x h

Fig. 14.1: How to derive the area of a parallelogram

Math Note

Area is the amount of two-dimensional space that a shape takes up. It can be thought of as a footprint of the shape. Area is typically measured in square units, even if the shape isn't square. These units can be any size but in general they are usually 1 cm² or 1 inch². To measure the area of the shape, divide it into small squares and count the number of square units.

A rectangle is a basic shape to start with for area determination. Rectangles can be thought of as containing rows and columns and area can be found by either counting the number of square units contained within or by multiplying the number of rows by the number of columns. The formula of (base x height) is just the number of rows multiplied by the number of columns. The formula is also denoted as (length x width). Any side of a polygon can be used as the base, but the height is the vertical distance between the base and the highest point in the figure. Height is always perpendicular to the base. Sometimes it's easier for the students to understand if the base to be used is oriented horizontally on the page. If the figure is a rectangle, then the height is just one of the sides adjacent to the base. Height must always be measured **perpendicular** to the base.

A parallelogram can be thought of as a hinged rectangle. If it is pushed to the side, the area inside gets smaller and smaller. The formula for calculating area of a parallelogram is the same as for a rectangle, base x height. One way to visualize this is by rearranging the parallelogram into a rectangle. The new rectangle has a height that is smaller than the corresponding side. So the area, which is equal to base x height, gets smaller as the height decreases.

A parallelogram can be divided in half along a diagonal to form two triangles and the area of one triangle is just half the area of the parallelogram or ½ (base x height). If the parallelogram is a rectangle, then the triangle is a right triangle and the two nonhypotenuse sides can be the base and height (interchangeably). The height of a non-right triangle is just the distance between the vertex opposite the base and the base. Any side can be the base and the height is determined accordingly.

In order to derive the formula for a trapezoid, the trapezoid can be doubled by flipping a second copy of it and sliding the two together to make a parallelogram. The area of the parallelogram is then the sum of the bases multiplied by the height, and the area of the trapezoid is half of this or $\frac{1}{2}(B_1 + B_2)$ x height.

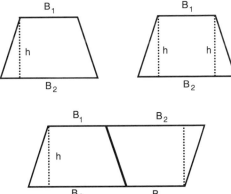

Fig. 14.2: How to derive the area of a trapezoid

Math Note (continued)

Even a circle can be divided into many small triangles and area estimated by laying out the triangles. The smaller the triangle, the better the estimate. This can be visualized by inscribing a polygon inside the circle and increasing the number of sides of the polygon. Then each side of the polygon becomes the base of a triangle. The area is then just the radius (which is now height) times the base (which is half the circumference). Since the circumference of a circle is equal to 2 x π x radius (C = $2\pi r$) and diameter = 2 x r, the area is just π x r x r. Remember that π is approximately 3.14159.

$$C = 2\pi r = \pi d \text{ and } A = \pi r \times r = \pi r^2$$

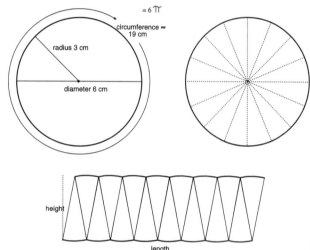

Fig. 14.3: How to derive the area of a circle

Exploration 2: Triangle

1. Each pair of students should have a piece of graph paper, scissors, and a ruler. Hand out the worksheet Three Different Sized Triangles to each pair of students.

2. **Challenge.** As in the previous exercise, ask the students to use the materials provided to determine the area formula of a triangle.

    Solution: Each rectangle can be divided along the diagonal, forming two congruent triangles. The students should see that one triangle equals half a rectangle. Since the area of a rectangle is b x h, the area of a triangle is ¹/₂ (b x h).

3. **Discuss.** Have several students show on the overhead how they arrived at their conclusions.

4. If students are having difficulty, use the transparency How to Derive the Area of a Triangle to show how to divide the rectangles into two equal triangles. Emphasize that the height of the triangle is the perpendicular distance between the base and the vertice opposite the base.

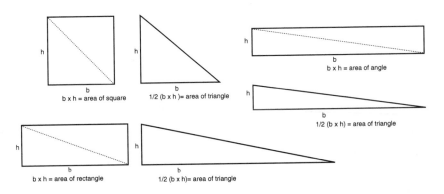

Fig. 14.4: How to derive the area of a triangle

Note: To wrap up the explorations, have students construct a poster(s) showing how to derive the different area formulas. Encourage students to use their own words on the poster(s).

Math Note

Notice that the formula for the area of a triangle is a product of three values: ¹/₂, base, and height. This can be written as a division problem as well:

$$\frac{b \times h}{2}$$

Keep in mind that multiplying these values follows the associative rule, not the distributive rule. In other words, you can multiply the three values in any order, but you cannot multiply the ¹/₂ by both the *b* and the *h* separately. So you can multiply ¹/₂ and b and then multiply the result by *h* or you can multiply ¹/₂ and *h* and then multiply the result by *b* or lastly you can multiply *h* and *b* and then multiply the result by ¹/₂.

How to Derive the Area of a Parallelogram

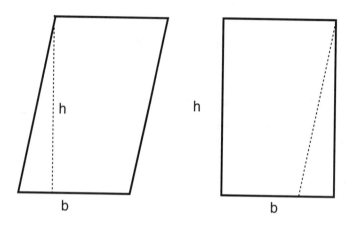

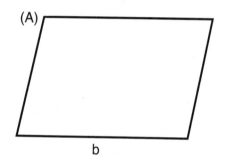

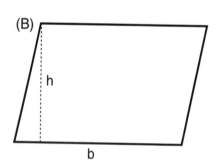

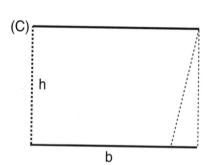

Area of a parallelogram = b x h
Area of a rectangle = l x w

How to Derive the Area of a Triangle

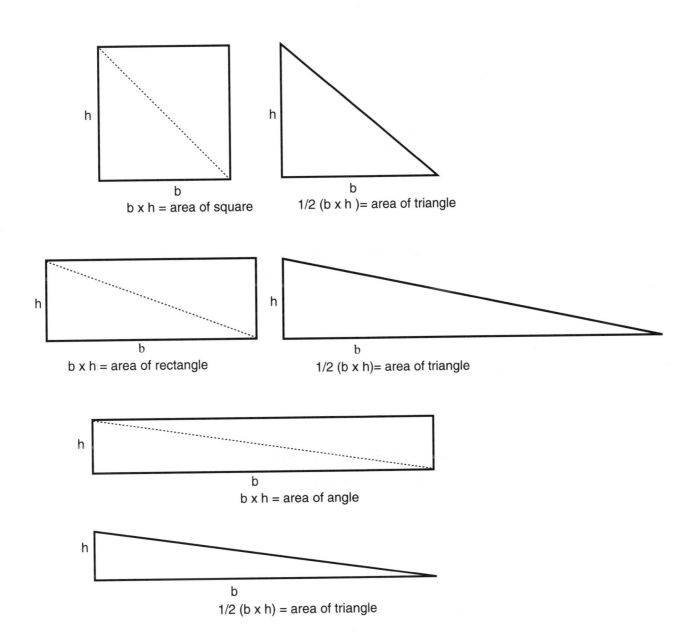

b x h = area of square

1/2 (b x h)= area of triangle

b x h = area of rectangle

1/2 (b x h)= area of triangle

b x h = area of angle

1/2 (b x h) = area of triangle

Three Different Sized Triangles

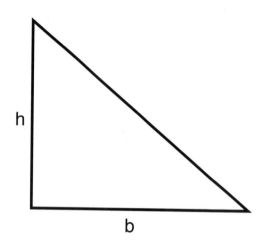

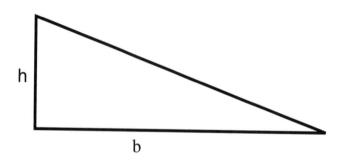

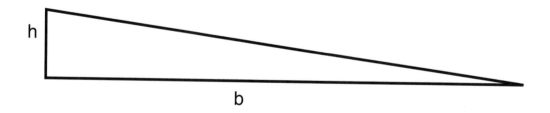

How to Derive the Area of a Trapezoid

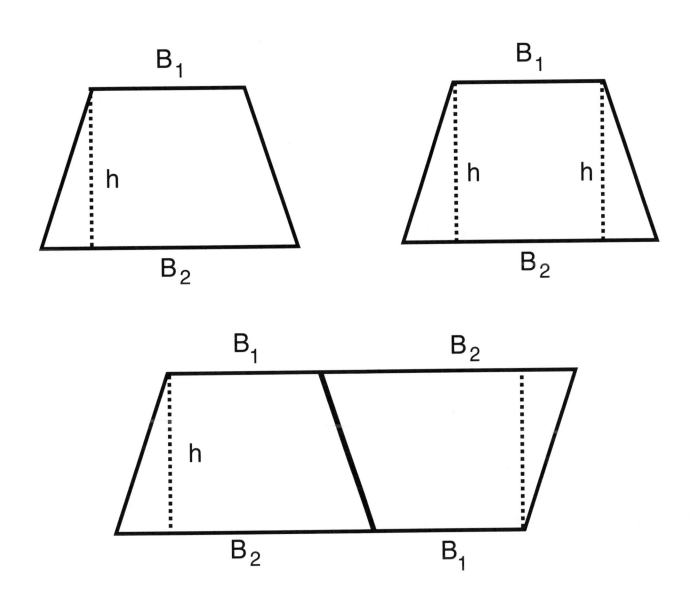

Practice Activity

1. Draw a square with a perimeter of 12 cm. Label the lengths of the sides. Find its area.

2. The area of a square is 64 cm². Draw the square and find its perimeter.

3. Find the area of the shaded region of this rectangle.

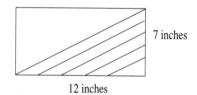

7 inches

12 inches

Explain how you found the area of the shaded region

4. Find the area of this trapezoid.

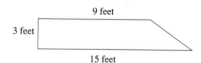

9 feet

3 feet

15 feet

Explain or illustrate how you found the area of this trapezoid.

5. Draw and label the base and height of two different rectangles that have an area of 24 in².

6. Draw and label a rectangle and a parallelogram that each have an area of 60 cm².

7. Find the perimeter of this triangle. Draw a different triangle with the same perimeter.

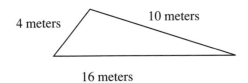

4 meters

10 meters

16 meters

8. Find the area of this right triangle. Draw another right triangle with the same area.

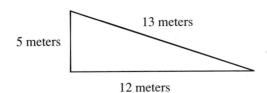

5 meters

13 meters

12 meters

9. What is the perimeter of this trapezoid?

    What is the height of this trapezoid?

    What is the area of the trapezoid?

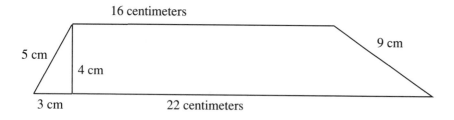

    Show your work.

10. A parallelogram and a rectangle have the same length and the same height. Are the following statements true or false?

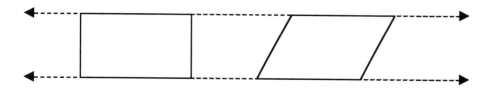

    a. The parallelogram and the rectangle have the same area.

    b. The parallelogram and the rectangle have the same perimeter.

Explain:

11. Some kids at school want to paint a basketball court. This is a sketch of their plan.

What is the total area they will paint with black paint?

What is the area of the basketball court?

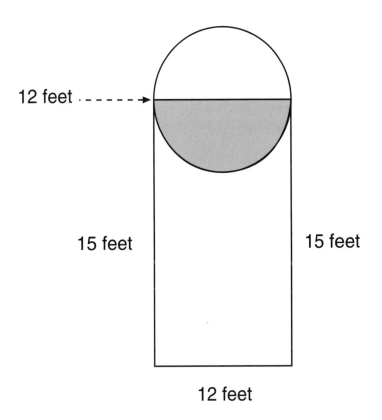

12 feet

15 feet   15 feet

12 feet

Hints:

What is the radius of the circle?

What is the circumference of the circle?

What is the area of half of the circle?

What is the perimeter of the rectangle?

What is the area of the rectangle?

Practice Activity Answer Key

1. Must be a square with all sides of 3 cm. Area is 9 sq cm.

2. Must be a square with all sides of 8 cm. Perimeter is 32 cm.

3. Find the area of the rectangle: it is 12 x 7 = 84 square inches. So, the area of the shaded region in half of that or 42 square inches.

4. Draw a perpendicular line from the end of the 9 ft base on top to the bottom base. Then we have a rectangle and a triangle. Since we know how to find the area of each, we will calculate them separately and then add them together. The area of the rectangle is 9*3 = 27 sq. ft. The triangle has a base of (15 – 9) = 6 ft. and a height of 3 ft. so the area is ½ x 6 x 3 or 9 sq. ft. The trapezoid has a total area of 27 + 9 = 36 sq. ft.

5. The rectangles must be different and the length and width must multiply to 24, so 1 x 24, 2 x 12, 3 x 8, 4 x 6, etc.

6. The rectangle and the parallelogram should have the same base and height: multiples of 60 (2 x 30, 4 x 15, etc). Make sure the height is labeled correctly for the parallelogram.

7. P = 30 m. Any other triangle with sum of sides equaling 30 m is fine.

8. A= ½ x 12 x 5 = 30 m² Any other triangle with the same area is fine: switching the base and height works or using 6 and 10 or 4 and 15 in place of the 12 and 5 works.

9. P = 5 + 3 + 22 + 9 + 16 = 55 cm. H = 4 cm. A = ½ x 3 x 4 + 16 x 4 + ½ x 8 x 4 =

    6 + 64 + 16 = 86 sq. cm.

10. (a) True since A = base x height.

    (b) False. The parallelogram will have a larger perimeter. To see this, draw in the height defined as the perpendicular distance. This is now the leg of a triangle and the hypotenuse is part of the perimeter. Since the hypotenuse of a right triangle is always longer than the legs, the perimeter will be larger than the perimeter of the rectangle.

11. Radius: 6 feet

    Circumference: 2 x pi x *r* = 2 *3.14*6ft = 37.68 ft.

    Area of half the circle: ½ x pi x *r* x *r* = 56.52 sq. ft.

    Perimeter of rectangle: 12 x 2 + 15 x 2 = 54 ft.

    Area of rectangle: 12 x 15 = 180 sq. ft.

    Total area to paint black is half of the area of the circle: 56.52 sq. ft.

    Area of the basketball court is the area of the rectangle and the area of half of the circle: 180 + 56.52 = 236.52 sq. ft.

Activity 15:
Area Held Constant with Perimeter Changing

Past investigations should have shown the students that perimeter is a linear function. That is, perimeter is the sum of the lengths of the sides, or A + B + C + D, in the case of a rectangle.

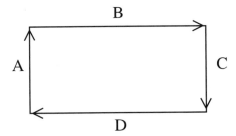

Fig. 15.1: Perimeter is a linear function

Students should have also learned that area is the space within the boundary. For example, the rectangle shown below has dimensions of 4 cm and 8 cm, and its area (4 cm x 8 cm) is 32 sq centimeters.

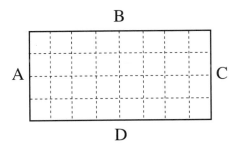

Fig. 15.2: Area measures space in square units

In addition, students have been investigating the relationship between perimeter and area when perimeter is held constant. Students have examined this relationship for different shapes such as triangles, parallelograms, and various-sized rectangles. Students have learned that area increases in size as various shapes approximate a circle. For various rectangles, students have observed that as the relationship between length and width become equal, as in the case of a square, the area increases.

Today's math challenge has students investigating the following problem: What happens to perimeter if area is held constant? By investigating various dimensions of perimeter and area, students will gain a deeper understanding of the relationship between perimeter and area. This is a good place for students to practice their problem-solving skills. See Problem-Solving Approach on page 6.

Goal

- To understand how perimeter can change when area is held constant

Materials

- Transparency, Solution to the Tiles Arrangement
- Worksheet, Cut-out Tiles (one per pair of students)
- Worksheet, Cm Graph Paper (one per pair of students; found on page 200)
- Scissors
- Ruler (one per pair of students)
- Student journals

Instructions

1. Pose the following situation to your students. A father and son are building the floor of a shed. They have a number of different sized tiles to lay out for the floor:

   - Four tiles with the dimensions: 4 cm x 1 cm:

   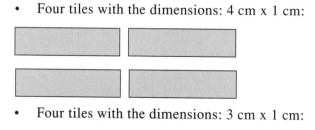

   - Four tiles with the dimensions: 3 cm x 1 cm:

   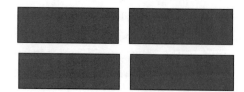

- Two tiles with the dimensions 2 cm x 1 cm:

- Four tiles with the dimensions: 1 cm x 1 cm:

After the tiles are laid out, the father and son will need to put a wood strip around the perimeter of the floor. The strip is very expensive, $1.25 per cm, so they agree that they want the area of the flooring to have the least perimeter. The dad says that it doesn't matter how the tiles are placed, but the son disagrees and says that the way it is laid out can affect perimeter. Ask your students to make conjectures about whether it matters how the flooring is laid out.

2. **Challenge.** To further explore this question, have students work in pairs. Hand out the Cut-out Tiles worksheet, graph paper, scissors, and ruler. Ask students to cut out the tiles and arrange them in such a way on the graph paper in order to determine the best layout. When they think they have the answer, they should note the area and perimeter of their shape. Then, they can calculate the cost of the wood strip that borders the tiles. Ask students to write their answers for the area, perimeter, and cost of the wood strip in their journals.

3. **Discuss.** Ask students to present their findings and how they arrived at their answers. After all pairs have presented, you may want to share the Solution to the Tiles Arrangement transparency (Fig. 15.3) if this arrangement was not presented yet.

Math Note

When students are solving the tile problem, they have an opportunity to find the maximum or minimum perimeter of a figure when the area is held constant. Again, this process is counterintuitive to many people. How can the perimeter change, even though the number of tiles (or area) stays the same? Students have the opportunity to construct a variety of designs and to determine which factors influence perimeter.

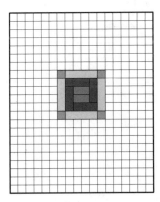

Fig. 15.3: Solution to the tiles arrangement

Cut-out Tiles

Solution to the Tiles Arrangement

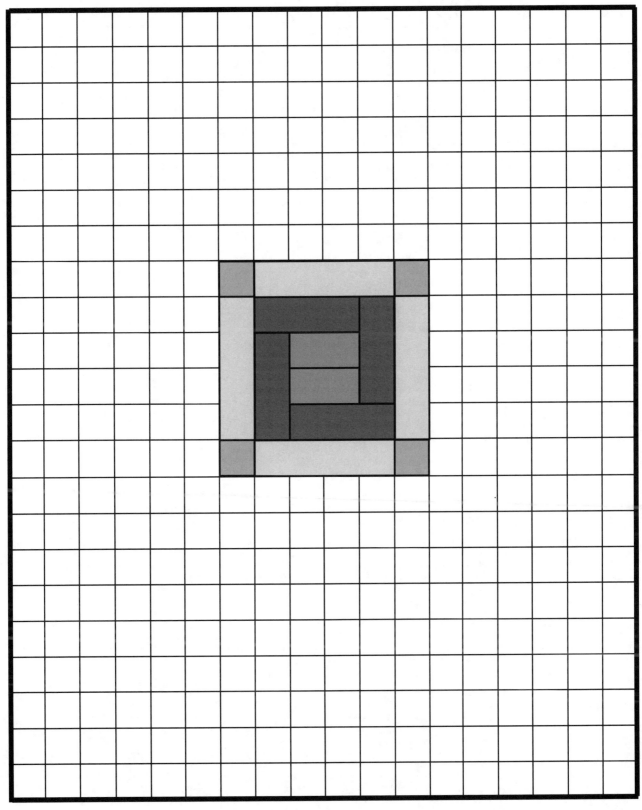

Activity 16:
Shape and Strength[*]

In the activity that follows, students explore the relationship between the geometrical shape of objects and their strength, since differently shaped fish rack supports lend greater or lesser stability to a fish rack. Students will notice that when paper is unfolded it cannot support any weight. However, when it has just one fold in it the paper becomes stronger. In its folded state it can be imagined as triangular.

In the remaining activities of the module students explore the strength of triangular prisms and rectangular prisms as supports for fish racks. They will notice that given the materials used the triangular prism is stronger.

Goals

- To explore ways of increasing the strength of a sheet of paper

- To predict and explain how the shape of paper affects its ability to support weight

- To investigate the properties of shape that affect strength

Materials

- A lightweight book (one per pair of students)
- Heavy books used to form an 8-inch (20 cm) gap (two per pair of students)
- Coin (one per pair of students)
- Paper (11 x 16 inches or 28 x 41 cm) (one sheet per pair of students)
- Student journals

Instructions

1. **Demonstrate.** Show students a piece of 11 x 16 inch (28 x 41 cm) paper. Ask them, "How strong do you think this paper is? Can it even support its own weight?" Try to stand the paper on its edge. Let go of the paper so that it falls. Next, hold the paper in one hand. Do not allow the paper to curve, dip, or bend. Then, place a coin on the pa-

[*] Mario Salvadori (1990). *The Art of Construction*. Chicago, IL: Chicago Review Press.

per. Again, make sure that the paper has no bend in it. If the paper is held flat, the coin will fall, and the paper will not be able to support the coin's weight (Fig. 16.1).

Fig. 16.1: A flat piece of paper cannot hold the coin

2. Now, have students work in pairs. Hand out a sheet of paper and a coin to each pair. Ask them to come up with a way to make the paper hold the coin. They can only hold the paper with one hand. The solution (don't tell them—let them figure it out!) is to bend the paper or fold it in half. The folded shape will support a coin (Fig. 16.2).

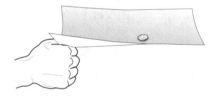

Fig. 16.2: A bent piece of paper can hold the coin

3. Have different pairs share their solutions.

4. **Challenge.** Now ask the students, "Can this piece of paper support a lightweight book?" Hand out journals, one lightweight book and two heavier ones to each pair of students. Tell them they must find a way to make the paper support the lightweight book using only the materials provided them. Explain the rules of this game.
   • One sheet of paper must support a lightweight book;
   • The paper must span 6 inches (15 cm);
   • The paper must not reinforce itself; in other words, the paper may not be folded completely over, so that two halves are touching.

5. After ten minutes ask students to note in their journals the strategies or designs that were successful and unsuccessful. Have them sketch the shape of the successful strategies. Have them answer the questions, "Are you surprised by the strength of paper? Could it hold more than its own weight? What seems to have made the difference in its ability to support weight?"

6. **Discuss.** Have students discuss their findings with the class.

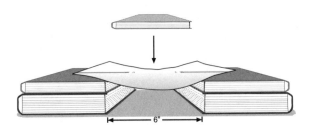

Fig. 16.3: When the paper is lying flat, it cannot support the book

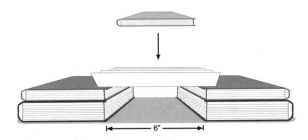

Fig. 16.4: When the paper is folded in an accordian fashion, it can hold the weight of the book

Teacher Note

The solution (again, let them figure it out on their own!) is to fold the paper into an accordion shape. Placed on top of two heavy books with a span of at least six inches, the folded paper should be able to support the lightweight book. The reason why the accordion is stronger has to do with its triangular shape. In Activity 17, as students experiment with different kinds of fish rack support structures, they will again discover the superior strength of the triangular form.

Activity 17:
Strength of Fish Rack Support Structures

In previous lessons, students have learned about the importance of a rectangular base for constructing a stable fish rack and about the relationship between perimeter and area when the perimeter is held constant. Different shapes with the same perimeter have different areas. Students have also learned that, when constructing a fish rack, both common sense and everyday mathematical criteria influence decision-making.

In today's lesson, students will explore the strength of the support structures used in two types of temporary fish racks: rectangular and triangular. Further, students will investigate the strength of three basic design features: a triangular prism (or tetrahedron) associated with the temporary fish rack, a pyramid, and a cube. By constructing simple models, students will test the strength of these three designs.

Goals

- To determine which shape is able to support the most weight by comparing a triangular prism (tetrahedron), a pyramid, and a cube

- To create and analyze three-dimensional objects that model real life situations

Materials

- Transparency, Two Styles of Temporary Fish Racks
- Transparency, Three Types of Support Structures
- Transparency, Support Structure Table
- Worksheet, Rules for Building a Fish Rack (one per group of students)
- Gumdrops (32 per group of students)
- Toothpicks (48 per group of students)
- If gumdrops and toothpicks aren't available, use paper clips (ninety-six per group of students) and straws (forty-eight per group of students)
- Weights (fishline sinkers) of one to five ounces for a total of 36 ounces (28 to 142 g, total 1,020 g)
- Twigs (five per group) or skewers (five per group of students)

- Plumb line (self-made from string and fishing weight, one per group of students)
- Ruler
- Student journals

Duration

- One to two class periods.

Vocabulary

- Cube—a solid with six equal square sides.
- Pyramid—any square structure with a square base and four sloping, triangular sides meeting at the top.
- Triangular prism or tetrahedron—a solid figure whose bases are congruent, parallel triangles and whose other faces are parallelograms.

Instructions

1. Show the transparency of the Two Styles of Temporary Fish Racks.

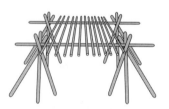   

A triangular fish rack   *A rectangular fish rack*

Fig. 17.1: Styles of temporary fish racks

2. Show the transparency of Three Types of Support Structures (triangular prism, pyramid, and cube). Hand out the journals, and have the students make conjectures in their journals about which one of these styles will be able to support the most weight and why.

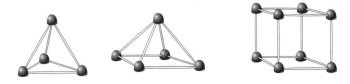

Fig. 17.2: Three types of support structures

3. **Challenge.** Have the students work in groups of three or four. Hand out the gumdrops and toothpicks (or the paper clips and straws). Allow them approximately fifteen minutes to build the three kinds of support structures. Their goal is to decide which of the three structures is the strongest or most stable - the tetrahedron, pyramid, or cube. If students are using paper clips and straws, three or more clips (depending on the shape being built) fastened together form the vertices. The clips stuff easily inside each straw.

Fig. 17.3: Student building a support structure

Fig. 17.4: A cube is less stable than a prism. This cube is leaning to one side

Fig. 17.5: A more stable structure than the cube

Teacher Note

After your students observe the strength of a triangular support structure, ask them where else they have seen this support structure used. Show them pictures of trusses, bridge supports, and other structures that use or incorporate triangular supports. Point out that in Activity 16 the sheet of paper folded into an accordion fashion, which was stronger than the flat sheet, was essentially a series of triangles.

4. Have students share their conclusions and reasoning with the rest of the class.

5. Since the Yup'ik often do not have access to abundant resources, they try to build their fish racks using the least amount of materials possible. Have students investigate with the three support structures to determine the one that uses the fewest materials.

6. **Discuss.** Have students discuss their solutions with the class. You may want to use the transparency Support Structure Table to aid the discussion. Ask the students, "Is the strongest structure also the most efficient? Does this surprise you?"

    Note: If time is running out, save the remainder of this activity for the next class period. Begin the next class period with a quick review of yesterday's findings.

7. Hand out worksheet Rules for Building a Fish Rack, the twigs (or skewers) and weights to each group. Explain to students that they are going to experiment building an entire fish rack model consisting of four support structures, two support beams (twigs or skewers), and three poles (twigs or skewers). (Note that the example shown in Fig. 17.6 has four support structures, two support beams, and only one pole.) They must choose one of the three types of support structures created earlier. Additionally their fish racks must hold at least 18 ounces (510 g) representing a scaled down weight of fish needed in order to meet the food needs of a family.

8. **Challenge.** After the students have built their four support structures, have them lay the two twig support beams across the support structures and one twig pole across them. Have them hang three one-ounce weights on the pole. If the structure holds, they can add the remaining two poles to the rack and three one-ounce weights to each pole. If the rack continues to hold, they can replace the one-ounce weights with two-ounce weights for a total of eighteen ounces. If the rack still looks good, students can continue adding weights. Each group should move from fish rack to fish rack, testing strength using the "fish'" weights.

    An additional criterion allows for a final test of stability. Have the students make a plumb line by attaching a weight to a string. Hang the plumb line from one of the poles when the whole structure is holding 20 ounces (567 g). The more unstable the structure, the more off-kilter it will look compared to the plumb line. Students may check the stability of their rack again at 25 ounces (709 g) and 30 ounces (851 g).

9. Have students write or draw observations in their journals. Encourage them to include the amount of material used, what happens to the poles when weight is added, and any proof to previous conjectures.

10. **Discuss.** Have a few students report their findings to the class and discuss stability, strength, and any difficulties they encountered in building the structures.

Fig. 17.6: Leah Lipka testing her design

Two Styles of Temporary Fish Racks

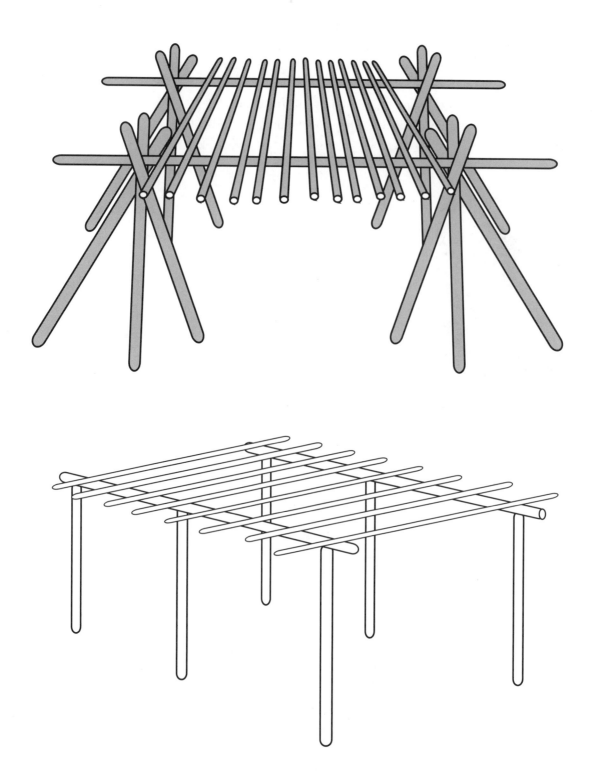

Blackline Master

Three Types of Support Structures

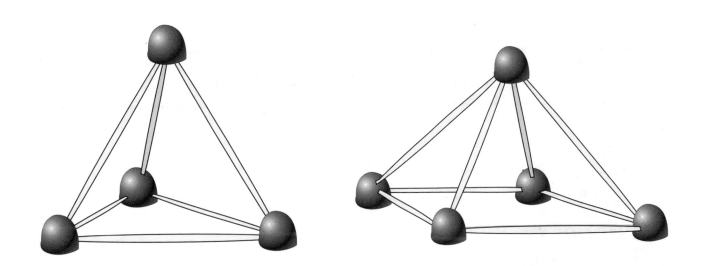

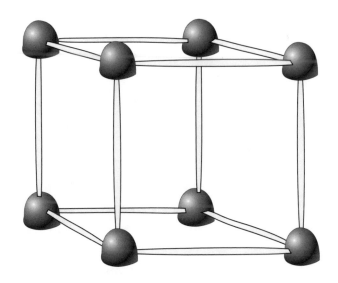

Support Structure Table

	Tetrahedron	Pyramid	Cube
Number of Toothpicks			
Number of Gumdrops			

Rules for Building a Fish Rack

- The goal is to create a fish rack model that holds the most weight but uses the least amount of supplies.

- Each group receives 32 gumdrops, 48 toothpicks, and 5 twigs or skewers for building material. Alternatively, 96 paper clips, 48 straws, and 5 twigs or skewers could be used.

- Only four support structures can be used. The support structures must be one of three types: tetrahedron, pyramid, or cube.

- The gap between support structures needs to be between 6 and 8 inches (15 to 20 cm).

- The support structures must hold two support beams.

- The support beams must hold three poles. The poles will extend from one support beam to another.

- The total fish rack model must hold **at least** 18 ounces (510 g). The weights should be placed hanging from the poles only.

Activity 18:
Constructing a Fish Rack

During this module, your class has explored many mathematical concepts as they built a fish rack—perimeter, area, and strength of various shapes. They also took into account practical and cultural considerations as they worked on their fish racks such as the fact that rectangular drying racks are easier to build than circular ones given that wood, the prime building material used by the Yup'ik, does not bend easily. In today's activity, your students are encouraged to be creative when building a new fish rack while at the same time considering everything they have learned—maximizing the strength of materials and shape, optimizing the area of the drying rack, and being efficient with the materials at hand.

If elders are available, this would be an excellent time to invite them into the classroom to assist your students. This is also an excellent time to have the students' work (posters, journals, models) displayed and shared with the families and community.

Goals

- To use materials in a creative manner when building a fish rack

- To apply knowledge of strength of design and efficient use of materials and space when constructing a fish rack

Materials

- Transparency, Various Fish Rack Designs
- Worksheet Cm Graph Paper (two sheets per group of students; found on page 200)
- Worksheet, Rules for Fish Rack Building Contest (one per group of students)
- Toothpicks (48 per group of students)
- Gumdrops (32 per group of students)
- As in the last activity, teacher can substitute paper clips and straws for gumdrops and toothpicks, if necessary
- Twigs or skewers (five per group of students)
- Ruler (one per group of students)
- One- and two-ounce weights (30 to 50 ounces) (28 to 56 g weights; 851 to 1,418 g)
- Student journals

Instructions

1. **Review.** Show transparency of Various Fish Rack Designs.

Fig. 18.1: Various Athabaskan fish rack designs

2. Have your students work in groups of four, or ideally two, if there are enough materials. Hand out Cm Graph Paper and rulers.

3. **Challenge.** Pose the following activity to students. Design a fish rack on graph paper that incorporates everything you have learned during the past week. In other words, you should design a structure that holds a lot of salmon, uses materials efficiently, and is strong and stable. At the same time, try to be creative and come up with some new designs, something that perhaps could be used for multiple purposes and in other seasons. Ask students: "What other things could a fish rack be used for?" List the student's responses on the board. Give students fifteen minutes to design their new fish rack.

4. To each team, hand out Rules for Fish Rack Building Contest, gumdrops, toothpicks (or paper clips and straws), and twigs. Allow students thirty minutes to build their fish racks. Have the weights available if students need to test the strength of their models.

5. Hold a contest. Scoring will take place in two categories: Strength and Creativity. On a sheet of paper score the strength of each fish rack by giving a half point for every ounce up to 30 ounces (851 g). Allow an additional five points for a fish rack design that can hold 40 ounces (1,134 g). Thus the maximum number of points in the strength category is twenty.

6. Ask students to circulate around the room to view all the designs. Have them rank each model based on creativity, by writing down a number from one to five. A value of one means least creative and a value of five means most creative. If elders or others are visiting, allow them to vote as well. Average the values for creativity.

7. Total up the scores for each fish rack model by combining the strength points and the average creativity points. The fish rack design to win the contest should be closest to the maximum value of twenty-five points.

8. To conclude the lesson, read the radio announcement from Alaska Department of Fish and Game. Students do not need to respond to this announcement. Its purpose is only to imitate what happens in real life, to conjure up the excitement and high anticipation that people feel on the day before fishing begins.

9. **Debrief.** Have the students discuss the different creative uses, interesting designs, and the relationship between design strength and stability of their fish racks.

10. Conclude the module with a discussion on students' impressions of the mathematics needed or used in building fish racks. Provide time for students to complete their journals and then collect them for assessment.

Radio Announcement

This is KYUK, Bethel, Alaska with an emergency order from the Alaska Department of Fish and Game. The number of salmon entering the Kuskokwim River is sufficiently large to allow for commercial and subsistence fishing. Fishermen, please standby for the opening.

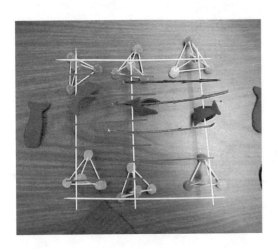

Fig. 18.2: An example of a complete fish rack with six support structures, two beams, and three poles

Looking Ahead

Students have now begun the process of connecting culture and math through mathematical modeling. Starting with a real-world situation— the need to build a fish rack—students investigated the mathematics required to understand the functions and designs of various fish racks and used the cultural, physical, and mathematical information to design their own fish racks. Hopefully they discovered other interesting facts throughout the process. They may have further ideas of how to continue to improve their models. Other supplemental modules can now be used to provide them with more information allowing students to further understand other aspects needed to improve and revise their fish rack models.

Various Fish Rack Designs

Athabaskan Fish Rack

Yup'ik Fish Rack

Athabaskan Fish Rack

Blackline Master

Rules for Fish Rack Building Contest

- The goal is to design and build a new and creative fish rack model that holds the most weight but uses the least amount of supplies.

- Each group receives 32 gumdrops, 48 toothpicks, and 5 twigs or skewers for building material. Alternatively, 96 paper clips, 48 straws, and 5 twigs or skewers could be used.

- Any number of support structures, support beams, and poles can be used. However, the poles must be at least $\frac{1}{2}$ inch (1.27 cm) apart and at least 4 inches (10 cm) off the ground.

- The total fish rack model must hold **at least** fifteen 2-ounce (56 g) weights. Each 2-ounce weight represents a 20-pound (9 kg) king salmon.

- Each fish rack model will be scored in two categories: strength and creativity. Strength is scored up to twenty points and creativity up to five points. In the strength category, a half point for every ounce up to 20 ounces (567 g) is given. An additional five points is given if the fish rack can hold 40 ounces (1,134 g). Creativity is based on an average value of votes from all the students with a maximum of five points.

Cm Graph Paper